# SpringerBriefs in Computer Science

*Series Editors*
Stan Zdonik
Peng Ning
Shashi Shekhar
Jonathan Katz
Xindong Wu
Lakhmi C. Jain
David Padua
Xuemin Shen
Borko Furht

For further volumes:
http://www.springer.com/series/10028

Sergio Escalera · Xavier Baró
Oriol Pujol · Jordi Vitrià
Petia Radeva

# Traffic-Sign Recognition Systems

Dr. Sergio Escalera
Department of Applied Mathematics
  and Analysis
University of Barcelona
Gran Via de les Corts Catalanes 585
08007 Barcelona
Spain
e-mail: sergio@maia.ub.es

Dr. Xavier Baró
Department of Computer Science
Universitat Oberta de Catalunya
Rambla del Poblenou 158
Barcelona
Spain
e-mail: xavier.baro@cvc.uab.es

Dr. Oriol Pujol
Department of Applied Mathematics
  and Analysis
University of Barcelona
Gran Via de les Corts Catalanes 585
08007 Barcelona
Spain
e-mail: oriol.pujol@cvc.uab.es

Dr. Jordi Vitrià
Department of Applied Mathematics
  and Analysis
University of Barcelona
Gran Via de les Corts Catalanes 585
08007 Barcelona
Spain
e-mail: jordi.vitria@cvc.uab.es

Dr. Petia Radeva
Department of Applied Mathematics
  and Analysis
University of Barcelona
Gran Via de les Corts Catalanes 585
08007 Barcelona
Spain
e-mail: petia@cvc.uab.es

ISSN 2191-5768
ISBN 978-1-4471-2244-9
DOI 10.1007/978-1-4471-2245-6
Springer London Dordrecht Heidelberg New York

e-ISSN 2191-5776
e-ISBN 978-1-4471-2245-6

British Library Cataloguing in Publication Data
A catalogue record for this book is available from the British Library

Library of Congress Control Number: 2011936533

*Cover design:* eStudio Calamar, Berlin/Figueres

Printed on acid-free paper

Springer is part of Springer Science+Business Media (www.springer.com)

# Contents

# Chapter 1
# Introduction

**Abstract** In recent years, the car industry has pushed forward large-scale research and industrial projects in Japan, the US and Europe related to the development of assisted driving technologies, thus allowing a real technology transfer from research to market. Several of these technologies are related to the problem of automatic traffic sign recognition, which has reached a certain level of maturity from a scientific point of view. Nevertheless, in spite of the fact that the most advanced cars have been equipped with these systems, at present, human drivers are still the main actors for ensuring safety in the traffic environment. Limitations for detecting and recognizing traffic signs can be grouped into four topics: Lighting conditions, environment clutter, sign variability, and data acquisition. In the following chapters, we will describe a full generic approach to the detection and recognition of traffic signs that cover state-of-the-art methodologies and deals with the aforementioned recognition problems.

**Keywords** Traffic sign detection · Traffic sign recognition · Color-based description · Shape-based description · Uncontrolled environments · Multi-class classification

Human beings have always needed to mark routes along their common pathways. Road signs are as old as roads themselves; the earliest ones were milestones, which indicated the distance or direction to important places. From the times of the tribune Gaius Gracchus, elected in 123 B.C., the Romans built tall marble columns all over the Empire showing the distance from Rome. To exploit the resources of the Empire, Gracchus made new roads throughout the country, repaired old ones, and erected the milestones which were arranged in a network with its center in a corner of the Forum in Rome. Within 200 km of this point, milestones showed the distance to Rome, and further afield milestones showed the distance from the nearest large town.

In the Middle Ages, multidirectional signs at intersections became common, giving directions to cities and towns. Traffic signs took on huge importance with the development of automobiles. One of the first modern-day road sign systems was devised by the Italian Touring Club in 1895. The basic patterns of most traffic

S. Escalera et al., *Traffic-Sign Recognition Systems*, SpringerBriefs in Computer Science, DOI: 10.1007/978-1-4471-2245-6_1, © Sergio Escalera 2011

signs were set by the International Road Congress held in Rome in 1908. In 1909, nine European governments agreed on the use of four pictorial symbols, indicating "bump", "curve", "intersection", and "level railroad crossing". The intensive work on international road signs carried out between 1926 and 1949 eventually led to the development of the European road sign system. By 1949 Europe had adopted a common system although the US government rejected it and designed a system of its own. In the 1960s, US signage began adopting international symbols into its system.

With the advances in computing and electronics, the idea of computer-based assistive technologies for drivers rapidly gained momentum. Technologies for anti-skid braking (ABS) and cruise control systems were quickly adopted by manufacturers, but more advanced systems, in spite of their potential benefits, have not been commercialized until recently. Examples of these systems are detection of driver fatigue or inattention, pedestrian spotting and blind spot checking and driver feedback for lane keeping, which all merge assistance and road context monitoring. One of the common features of these systems is that they rely on rich sensor data which is inherently imprecise, complex, and difficult to analyze. So the key to their success has been the development of robust methods to perceive the car environment.

Automatic traffic sign detection and recognition has now been successfully transferred from research to the market. Originally, this field of applied computer vision research was concerned with the automatic detection and classification of traffic signs in scene images acquired from a moving car. It is not difficult to see that a system of this kind can significantly increase driving safety and comfort, but this is not its only application: for instance, it can be used in a highway maintenance system to verify the presence and conditions of traffic signs. Recognition of road signs is a challenging problem that has engaged the Computer Vision community for more than 40 years. Significant breakthroughs were made in the 1980 and 1990s, when the problem of computer vision-based driver assistance began to be taken seriously for the first time. In recent years the car industry has pushed forward large-scale research and industrial projects in Japan, the US and Europe. Although with the latest technology cars carry automatic traffic sign detectors, at present it is still human drivers who have to recognize traffic signs and ensure safety in the traffic environment. The following applications are examples of automatic traffic sign recognition (the list is not exhaustive) [1]:

- *Assisted-driving application.* Automatic traffic signs recognition can help drivers in basic tasks warning them of situations of particular danger, assisting in controlling speed, "reading the text" on road signs [2], etc.
- *Constructing autonomous, intelligent vehicles.* In the near future, intelligent vehicles are expected to take advantage of automatic TS recognition systems and other functions such as detection of road lines, pedestrians, and other road obstacles. Autonomous intelligent vehicles should contain facilities for traffic detection and recognition. An example is the "Intelligent Stop & Go" system developed in the European Prometheus project [3] which constructs an intelligent vehicle that "keeps a constant distance from the vehicle in front (as a radar-based system would do), is able to follow the car in front, stop at red traffic lights and stop signs, give

way to other vehicles if necessary, and try to avoid unpredictable hazards, such as children running across the street".

- *Sign maintenance application.* Many road maintenance and other road inventory companies still inspect roads manually. Manual detection and recognition of traffic signs is a slow, expensive and tedious process because of the size of today's road networks (comprising millions of kilometers) and the high number of traffic signs per kilometer. Automating this process allows the replacement of human operators by automatic image processing and computer vision systems able to achieve faster and efficient results and drastically/significantly bring down their production cost.

Drivers, cyclists and pedestrians are the main users of traffic signs. For these reason, traffic signs were designed for optimal human detection and reading. Visibility design requirements ensure that the sign is visible by people of all age groups from an appropriate distance. Visibility also means that the sign has enough contrast with the background to be conspicuous and that the contents on the sign have sufficient contrast with the background of the sign. These characteristics make the problem less difficult than the general object recognition problem in computer vision, but there are nonetheless at least four sources of problems when detecting and recognizing traffic signs:

- *Lighting conditions.* Lighting differs according to the time of the day and season, weather conditions, and local variations such as the direction of light.
- *Environment clutter.* The presence of other objects—trees, pedestrians, other vehicles, billboards, and buildings—can cause partial occlusion and shadows.
- *Sign variability.* The sign installation and surface material can physically change over time, influenced by accidents and weather. Moreover, traffic signs exist in hundreds of variants that often do not comply with legally defined standards.
- *Data acquisition.* Images taken from the camera of a moving car often suffer from motion blur and car vibration.

In the following chapters, we will describe a full generic approach to the detection and recognition of traffic signs. The approach is based on the latest computer vision methods for object detection and on powerful methods for multiclass classification. It was originally developed for a mobile mapping application. The main aims were to robustly detect a set of different sign classes in real time and to classify each sign detected into a large, extensible set of classes. To address these problems, we developed several state of the art methods which can be used for different recognition problems. These methods are described in detail in the following pages. This book is divided into five chapters. Chapter 2 introduces the traffic sign detection and categorization problem. Chapter 3 focuses on the detection problem and presents some recent developments in this field. Chapter 4 surveys a specific methodology for the problem of traffic sign categorization, Error-Correcting Output Codes, and presents several algorithms. Chapter 5 shows experimental results for a mobile mapping application. Finally, Chap. 6 draws some conclusions about future lines of research and challenges for traffic sign recognition.

**Acknowledgments**  The authors would like to thank the people and organizations that have supported this study, and in particular Ramon Alamús, Ernest Bosch, Joan Casacuberta, Josep Lluís Colomer, Maria Pla, Santi Sànchez, Albert Serra and Julià Talaya from the Institut Cartogràfic de Catalunya for responding to our questions, making this research possible and providing us with a huge amount of high quality data for developing our methods.

# References

1. Jiménez, P.G., Maldonado, S., Gómez, H., Lafuente-Arroyo, S., López, F.: Traffic sign shape classification and localization based on the normalized FFT of the signature of blobs and 2D homographies. Signal Process. **88**, 2943–2955 (2008)
2. Wu, W., Chen, X., Yang, J.: Detection of text on road signs from video. IEEE Trans. Intell. Transp. Syst. **6**(4), 378–390 (2005)
3. Franke, W., Gavrila, D., Gorzig, S., Lindner, F., Paetzold, F., Wohler, Ch.: Autonomous driving goes downtown. IEEE on Intelligent Systems, pp. 40–48, Nov–Dec (1998)

# Chapter 2
# Background on Traffic Sign Detection and Recognition

**Abstract** The automatic sign detection and recognition has been converted to a real challenge for high performance of computer vision and machine learning techniques. Traffic sign analysis can be divided in three main problems: automatic location, detection and categorization of traffic signs. Basically, most of the approaches in locating and detecting of traffic signs are based on color information extraction. A natural question arises: which is the most proper color space to assure robust color analysis without influence of the exterior environment. Given the strong dependence on weather conditions, shadows and time of the day, some autors focus on the shape-based sign detection (e.g. Hough transform, ad-hoc models based on Canny edges or convex hulls). Recognition of traffic signs has been addressed by a large amount of classification techniques: from simple template matching (e.g. cross-correlation similarity), to sophisticated Machine learning techniques (e.g. suport vector machines, boosting, random forest, etc), are among strong candidates to assure straightforward outcome necessary for a real end-user system. Moreover, extending the traffic sign analysis from isolated frames to videos can allow to significantly reduce the number of false alarm ratio as well as to increase the precision and the accuracy of the detection and recognition process.

**Keywords** Traffic sign detection · Traffic sign recognition · Color-based description · Shape-based description · Uncontrolled · Environments · Multi-class classification

Recognition of road signs is a challenging problem that has engagedthe attention of the Computer Vision community for more than 30 years. According to Paclik [1], the first study of automatedroad sign recognition was reported in Japan in 1984. Since then, anumber of methods have been developed for road sign detection andidentification. For years, researchers have been addressingthe difficulties of detecting and recognizing traffic signs.

The most common automatic systems for traffic signs detection and recognitioncomprise one or two video cameras mounted on the front of the vehicle

S. Escalera et al., *Traffic-Sign Recognition Systems*, SpringerBriefs in Computer Science, DOI: 10.1007/978-1-4471-2245-6_2, © Sergio Escalera 2011

(e.g. a geovan). Recently, some geovans also have another camera at the rear and/or the side of the vehicle recording the signs behind or alongside the vehicle. The cars are fitted with a PC system for acquiring the videos, or specialized hardware for driving assistance applications.

Road signs have specific properties that distinguish them fromother outdoor objects. Operating systems for the automatic recognition of road signs are designed to identify these properties. Traffic sign recognition systems have three main parts:

1. Location of the region of interest and segmentation: usually, a number of binary masks are generated to separate the objects of interest from the background. Usually, color information is applied since traffic signs are characterized by a predetermined number of relatively constant colors (white, red, and blue). As a result, regions of interest are determined as connected components, some of which are traffic signs.
2. Detection by verification of the hypothesis of the presence of the sign: to detect signs most authors use knowledge of their shape (e.g. equilateral triangles, circles, etc.)
3. Categorization of the type of traffic sign: the final step is the recognition of the sign using a fixed database of all possible traffic sign models. Methods ranging from template matching to sophisticated machine learning apparatus can be used to achieve robust and efficient recognition of traffic signs.

The detection of the signs from outdoor images is the most complex step in the automatic traffic sign recognition system [2]. Many issues make theproblem of the automatic detection of traffic signs difficult (see Fig. 2.1) such as changeable light conditions which are difficult to control (lighting varies according to the time of the day, season, cloud cover and otherweather conditions); presence of other objects on the road (traffic signs are often surrounded by other objects producing partial occlusions, shadows, etc.); it is very difficult to generate all off-line models of all the possibilities since signs have a high number of degrees of freedom (their size depends on the camera distance and angle of views causing affine deformation; equally, age and accidents can also affect the signGs appearance). Hence, any robust automatic detection and recognition system must provide straightforward results that are not affected by perspective distortion, lighting changes, partial occlusions or shadows [3]. Ideally, the system should also provide additional information on the lack of visibility, poor conditions and poor placement of the traffic signs.

## 2.1 Color-Based Sign Detection

Sign detection using color is based on the five typical colors defined in standard traffic signs (red, blue, yellow, white and black). Most researchers look for robust color segmentation, paying special attention to non-homogeneous illumination, since errors in segmentation may be propagated in the following steps of the system. One of

**Fig. 2.1** A real outdoor scene of a road with traffic sign

the first attempts to construct a real-time system for automatic traffic sign recognition appears in Akatsuka et al. [4] where a look-up table in Nrgb color space is used in order to specifically design the segmentation of the speed limit signs. The authors in [5] studied the changes in traffic sign colors according to the time of the day (sunrise, midday, sunset). They deduced that the variation of the outdoor illumination does not significantly affect the RGB component differences of the colors of TSs, and proposed a simple algorithm for the segmentation of the images as a first step towards an automatic TS detection system. Zadeh et al. in [6] proposed a careful analysis of the nature of variations of pixel values of the same color in the RGB space and designed sub-spaces corresponding to the highest rate of variation of the traffic sign colors.The sub-spaces are defined as canonical regions placed on straight lines from RGB (0,0,0) to the combination of primary colors corresponding to the TSs. Other color appearance models have also been presented although they have received less attention. For example, Escalera et al. in [7] operated on the ratios between the intensity of a given channel and the sum of all RGB channel intensities. They pointed out that the RGB-HSV conversion formulas are non-linear and hence the computational cost involved is excessively high. Ritter et al. in [8, 9] combined color of image regions to create a specific code for traffic sign detection and then applied different shape filters to detect the TS presence within the region of interest. False color regions were filtered by using special look-up tables in the RGBcolor space.

A different approach was adopted in [10] where the authors trained scale-specific road sign detectors using Haar wavelet features parameterized by color. The best features were selected by a cascaded AdaBoost framework from a large space of features defined over multiple color representations: plain R, G, and B channels, normalized R, G, and B channels, and a gray-scale channel. In this way, the most suitable color representation wasinferred automatically from the data rather than arbitrarily chosen by the authors. Despite the excellent final results, one of the main drawbacks of these approaches is the high computational load that makes it difficult to produce a real-time system. As the authors note, for a $384 \times 288$ video resolution a processing speed of only 10 frames per second is achieved.

Among the studies in which the color information was used to detect the traffic signs, a significant amount of work can be found based on non-RGB color spaces. The Hue-Saturation-Value (HSV) color model was adopted because it is based on human color perception and is considered largely invariant to illumination changes. In [11] the authors defined sub-spaces limiting the color values of stop signs. Liu et. al. in [12] used color quantization in the HSV color model to find ROIs, followed by border tracing and ROI scaling. Piccioli et al. [13] defined the regions of interest by clusteringsmall blocks of the image where the number of pixels with a hue in an appropriate range exceeded a predetermined threshold.

The authors in [14] use a HSV model to classify the test sign images into several distinctive categories. Fang et. al. in [15] extract color features by a neural network. The authors in [16] presented a novel parallel segmentation algorithm called color structure code based on a hierarchical region growing on a special hexagonal topology that extracts sets of color regions (in the HSI color space) from theimages. The authors in [17] estimated the appearance of sign-characteristic colors independently from real-life images taken under different viewing conditions. They adopted the CIECAM97 color model to segment the images. An original and robust approach to color-based detection and segmentation of road signs using IHLS color space was also proposed in [18]. Both these studies considered device-independent color appearance models, which may be a better option than the standard device-dependent RGB model.

Recent work has recorded significant advances applying advanced machine learning techniques. Nguwi in [19] segment traffic signs pixels in YCbCr color space by using a multi-layer perceptron trained on traffic signs vs. non-traffic signs regions of interest. Fang et al. in [20] applied a Spatio-Temporal Attentional neural network to extract information of interest related to the formation of focuses of attention. Sign detection is obtained by analyzing the combination of color and edge information. The image features were learned by Configurable Adaptive Resonance Theory and Hetero-Associative Memory networks to classify the category and the object within that category.

A complete comparison between different segmentation techniques is presented by Gómez-Moreno in [21] where special attention is paid to the different color spaces to represent TS image features. The authors showed that the best methods are those that are normalized with respect to the illumination, such as RGB or Ohta Normalized, and, surprisingly, there is no improvement in the use of Hue Saturation Intensity spaces. In addition, using a LUT with a reduction in the less-significant bits improves speed, while maintaining quality of the TS segmentation. Applying a support vector machine, the authors obtain reasonable results although, as they admit, improvements in achromatic colors are still required in order to achieve the level of performance a real system needs.

On the other hand, color segmentation may suffer from various phenomena such as distance from the target, weather conditions, time of day, or reflectance of the signsĠ surfaces. Some authors have preferred a strictly colorless approach. They apply genetic algorithms [22] or distance transforms (DTs) [23]. In [24], the images were transformed using wavelets and classified by a Perceptron neural network.

Even though changes in lighting conditions affect the color information, color remains a useful clue for detecting and recognizing traffic signs. Moreover, signs may have very similar appearances and color may be a very important characteristic for distinguishing between them. When there is a large number of classes in the traffic sign database, color carries very valuable discriminative information which should be used whenever possible. Finally, we should not forget that in some countries, e.g. Japan, there are pairs of signs which differ only in terms of color. Thus, developing robust color models taking into account the variance of color appearance is of great interest for final automatic driving systems.

## 2.2 Shape-Based Sign Detection

Recent advances in object recognition open up great opportunities for robust traffic sign detection in uncontrolled environments. Still, challenges remain, such as the detection of traffic signs in cluttered scenes, in varying conditions of brightness and illumination, affine distortions according to the point of view, partial occlusions or even other signs and other information attached to traffic signs. Another additional difficulty is the simplicity of the shape of the traffic sign, which means that it can be easily confused with other objects or parts of objects. Depending on its distance from the acquisition system, the traffic signĠs size can vary and its spatial resolution may be very low (e.g. 30–40 pixels).

Given the regular geometric information provided by the traffic signs, one of the first attempts to address the problem was to apply Hough transform on the edge map of the region of interest [11]. To speed up the process Piccioli in [13] used color information to limit the region of interest followed by a geometrical analysis on the edge map to extract and detect circular and triangular shapes. After extracting straight lines using Canny edges the different segments of proper length and slope may be suitable for use as traffic signs. In [16] the authors propose a method that first segments the images based on their color and then applies a local and global growing technique to hierarchically organize the information and form the traffic sign candidates. Their convex hulls are compared to a predetermined set of basic traffic sign shapes to check that the region of interest represents a traffic sign. Moreover, the authors claim that the real-time performance they achieve makes the method very attractive for final integration in operating systems.

Again, machine learning approaches significantly improve the final results of traffic sign detection. In [7], the authors developed a simple approach based on color thresholding and shape analysis to detect the signs,followed by a neural network to classify them. In later work [3], they showed that the use of color LUTs in the HSI space to identify the regions of interest and genetic algorithms to detect the signs within the regions of interest produced much better final results. The main advantage of their approach based on genetic algorithms is that it allows for efficient traffic sign detection regardless of position, scale, rotation, partial occlusions, the presence of other objects, and variations in weather conditions. Final traffic sign recognition is achieved by aneural network. An alternative is presented by Gavrila et al. in [23] in which potential traffic signs are identified by a template-based correlation method using distance transforms,while the classification is based on radial basis function networks. A different machine learning approach is used in [25] where a support vector machine is responsible for segmenting the image in the RGB space followed by the detection of circular shapes, paying special attention to possible sign deformations.

## 2.3  Sign Recognition

Once the region of interest is determined and a traffic sign is detected, it should be recognized using a predetermined database of all the traffic signs in the system. Most of the state-of-the-art approaches can be divided into two strategies: template-based vs. classifier-based comparison. The most frequent similarity measure in traffic sign classification is normalized cross-correlation [13]. Here, a specific similarity measure between the gray-level region of interest and several templates of the traffic signs is estimated based on the normalized cross-correlation in order to identify the traffic sign. Using 60 circular signs and 47 triangular signs in their database, these authors report an accuracy of 98%.The main advantage of normalized cross-correlation isits simplicity, robustness to varying illumination conditions, and the ease of finding a statistical interpretation. It is also appealing from the point of view of implementation since it has been shown to be equivalent to an optical correlator [26]. Another template matching method can be observed in [27] who considered a database of 30 triangular signs and 10 circular signs and achieved an accuracy of 85%. Zadeh et al. in [6] presented an approach for model matching analyzing the area ratio of the colors in the regions of interest horizontally and vertically in order to differentiate between traffic signs with similar overall color ratios. The advantage of their approach is that the method is invariant to rotation and size of the region and so the number of potential models is substantially reduced, thus accelerating the systemĠs recognition time. Because of the global nature of template-based matching (e.g. cross-correlation similarity), the method may suffer from the presence of non-informative regions of interest pixels (e.g. due to occlusions). To cope with this problem, in [28] the authors propose a novel trainable similarity measure based on individual matches in a set of local image regions. Additionally, the set of regions relevant for a particular similarity measure can be refined by training procedures. A step forward in measuring the dissimilarity between different signs is presented by [29] where a special color distance transform enables robust comparison of discrete color image signs. The authors show that this method of feature selection combined with a one-vs-all nearest neighbor classifier performs better than alternatives like Principal Component Analysis or Adaboost offering adequate description of signs with little training effort.

The second group of approaches is based on more sophisticated machine learning techniques which in general achieve more robust final results when the images are analyzed under uncontrolled environments.The early work was based on neural networks such as the one presented by Krumbiegel et al. in [30] where a neural network is trained on the color, shape and texture of the traffic sign templates. Douvilee in [24] used amultilayer perceptron on the fast Fourier transform of the detected sign and a bank of filters, and found that a neural network achieves better results than the template matching procedure. Cyganek in [25] used two committee networks operating in the spatial domain and the log-polar representation. Each committee network was composed by several Hamming neural networks trained on a set of signs of reference. A san alternative, Nguwi et al. in [19] showed that a cascade of multilayer perceptron machines achieved better results than a support vector machine where Resilient Back propagation and Scaled Conjugate Gradient algorithms achieved a classification accuracy of 96% in near real time.

One of the main drawbacks of current methods for traffic sign recognition is the lack of a public domain database that contains enough examples of a wide set of traffic signs acquired in uncontrolled environments [2]. Most of the published works are presented on a limited number of signs with a small number of different examples. An exception is the study in [2] where a database of 1,500 road scene images is analyzed with traffic signs extracted and included in the board image data set and over 3,500 images of individual traffic sign boards. Images have been acquired from three European countries: the Czech Republic, Spain and the United Kingdom, and represent a great variability of illumination and meteorological conditions. In order to achieve robust results, a self-organizing map is used to detect potential road signs by analyzing the distribution of red pixels within the image. Traffic signs are detected from the distributions of the dark pixels in their pictograms. Following this, a hybrid system is introduced combining programmable hardware and neural networks for embedded machine vision leading to a robust and fast final prototype of the system and achieving very satisfactory results in near real time.

A real end-user system for traffic sign detection and recognition must offer high performance but should also be real-time. In [31] the authors apply the radial symmetry detector in order to discover the speed signs in urban scenarios and test it in a real environment. The detector is mounted inside a road vehicle and its performance, speed and stability are tested while the vehicle is moving. The detector is shown to run under a wide variety of visual conditions. Another study in which radial symmetry helps to achieve fast and robust detection is presented in [32]. The authors show that combining a Canny edge detector with the radial symmetry techniques and Adaboost as a classifier obtains very accurate final traffic sign recognition results in spite of the high variance of sign appearance due to noise, affine deformation, and reducedillumination.

Most studies on automatic detection and recognition of traffic signs are developed in a single frame. However, mobile mapping systems are also used to acquire videos or sequences of traffic scenes; thus, temporal information can prove very useful for increasing the accuracy of the detection and recognition process. In [15] the authors apply Kalman filters to track the signs until their size is large enough to ensure robust recognition results. A more recent study by the same authors [20] presents the evolution of the system based on a computational model of human visual recognition processing. The system consists of three basic parts: sensory, perceptual and conceptual analyzers. The sensory part extracts the spatio-temporal information from the video sequences. The information obtained is used by a spatio-temporal attentional neural network in the perceptual analyzer. This part decides whether the focus of attention corresponds to a horizontal projection of a road sign. The signs detected are normalized and correlated with all the prototypes previously stored in the traffic sign database. Excellent results have been achieved with tolerance of three pixels due to the spatio-temporal information embedded in the tracking system and the final recognition module.

# References

1. Paclik, P.: Road sign recognition survey. Online, http://euler.fd.cvut.cz/research/rs2/files/skoda-rs-survey.html
2. Prieto, M., Allen, A.: Using self-organizing maps in the detection and recognition of road signs. Image Vis. Comput. **27**, 673–683 (2009)
3. de la Escalera, A., Armingol, J., Mata, M.: Traffic sign recognition and analysis for intelligent vehicles. Image Vis. Comput. **21**, 247–258 (2003)
4. Akatsuka, H., Imai, S.: Road signposts recognition system. In: The International Conference on SAE Vehicle Highway Infrastructure: safety compatibility, pp. 189–196 (1987)
5. Benallal, M., Meunier, J.: Real-time color segmentation of road signs. In: Proceedings of the IEEE Canadian Conference on Electrical and Computer Engineering (CCGEI) (2003)
6. Suen, C.Y., Zadeh, M.M., Kasvand, T.: Localization and recognition of traffic road signs for automated vehicle control systems. In: Proceedings of the SPIE Intelligent system and automated manufacturing, pp. 272–282 (1998)
7. de la Escalera, A., Moreno, L.E., Salichs, M.A., Armingol, J.M.: Road traffic sign detection and classification. IEEE Trans. Ind. Electron. **44**((6), 848–859 (1997)
8. Ritter, W., Stein, F., Janssen, R.: Traffic sign recognition using colour information. Math. Comput. Model. **22**(4-7), 149–161 (1995)
9. Ghica, R., Lu, S., Yuan, X.: Recognition of traffic signs using a multilayer neural network. In: Proceedings of the Canadian Conference on Electrical and Computer Engineering (1994)
10. Bahlmann, C., Zhu, Y., Ramesh, V., Pellkofer, M., Koehler, T.: (2005) A system for traffic sign detection, tracking and recognition using color, shape, and motion information. In: Proceedings of the IEEE Intelligent Vehicles Symposium, pp. 255–260
11. Kehtarnavaz, N., Griswold, N.C., Kang, D.S.: Stop-sign recognition based on colour-shape processing. Machin. Vis. Appl. **6**, 206–208 (1993)
12. Liu, Y.S., Duh, D.J., Chen, S.Y., Liu, R.S., Hsieh, J.W.: Scale and skew-invariant road sign recognition. Int. J. Imaging Syst. Technol. **17**((1), 28–39 (2007)

13. Piccioli, G., De Micheli, E., Parodi, P., Campani, M.: Robust method for road sign detection and recognition. Image Vis. Comput. **14**(3), 209–223 (1996)
14. Paclik, P., Novovicova, J., Pudil, P., Somol, P.: Road signs classification using the laplace kernel classifier. Pattern Recognit. Lett. **21**(13-14), 1165–1173 (2000)
15. Fang, C.Y., Chen, S.W., Fuh, C.S.: Roadsign detection and tracking. IEEE Trans. Veh. Technol. **52**((5), 1329–1341 (2003)
16. Priese, L., Klieber, J., Lakmann, R., Rehrmann, V., Schian, R.: New results on traffic sign recognition. In: IEEE Proceedings of the Intelligent Vehicles Symposium, pp. 249–254 (1994)
17. Gao, X.W., Podladchikova, L., Shaposhnikov, D., Hong, K., Shevtsova, N.: Recognition of traffic signs based on their colour and shape features extracted using human vision models. J. Vis. Commun. Image Represent. **17**((4), 675–685 (2006)
18. Fleyeh, H.: Color detection and segmentation for road and traffic signs. Proc. IEEE Conf. Cybern. Intell. Syst. **2**, 809–814 (2004)
19. Nguwi, Y.Y., Kouzani, A.Z.: Detection and classification of road signs in natural environments. Neural Comput. Appl. **17**((3), 265–289 (2008)
20. Fang, C.Y., Fuh, C.S., Yen, P.S., Cherng, S., Chen, S.W.: An automatic road sign recognition system based on a computational model of human recognition processing. Comput. Vis. Image Underst. **96**((2), 237–268 (2004)
21. Gómez, H., Maldonado, S., Jiménez, P.G., Gómez, H., Lafuente-Arroyo, S.: Goal evaluation of segmentation for traffic sign recognition. IEEE Trans. Intell. Transp. Syst. **11**(4), 917–930 (2010)
22. Aoyagi, Y., Asakura, T.: A study on traffic sign recognition in scene image using genetic algorithms and neural networks. In: Proceedings of the 1996 IEEE IECON 22nd International Conference on Industrial Electronics Control and Instrumentation **3**, 1838–1843 (1996)
23. Gavrila, D.: Multi-feature hierarchical template matching using distance transforms. In: Proceedings of the IEEE International Conference on Pattern Recognition, pp. 439–444, Brisbane, Australia (1998)
24. Douville, P.: Real-time classification of traffic signs. Real-Time Imaging, **6**(3), 185–193 (2000)
25. Cyganek, B.: Circular road signs recognition with soft classifiers. Computer-Aided Eng. **14**((4), 323–343 (2007)
26. Guibert, L., Petillot, Y., de de la Bougrenet Tochnaye, J.L.: Real-time demonstration on an on-board nonlinear joint transform correlator system. Opt. Eng. **36**((3), 820–824 (1997)
27. Hsu, S.H., Huang, C.L.: Road sign detection and recognition using matching pursuit method. Image Vis. Comput. **19**, 119–129 (2001)
28. Paclik, P., Novovicova, J., Duin, R.: Building road-sign classifiers using a trainable similarity measure. IEEE Trans. Intell. Transp. Syst. **6**(3), 309–321 (2006)
29. Ruta, A., Li, Y., Liu, X.: Real-time traffic sign recognition from video by class-specific discriminative features. Pattern Recognit. **43**, 416–430 (2010)
30. Krumbiegel, D., Kraiss, K.-F., Schrieber, S.: A connectionist traffic sign recognition system for onboard driver information. In: Proceedings of the Fifth IFAC/IFIP/IFORS/IEA Symposium on Analysis, Design and Evaluation of Man-Machine Systems, pp. 201–206 (1992)
31. Barnes, N., Zelinsky, A., Fletcher, L.: Real-time speed sign detection using the radial symmetry detector. IEEE Trans. Intell. Transp. Syst. **9**(2), 322–332 (2008)
32. Escalera, S., Radeva, P. et al.: Fast greyscale road sign model matching and recognition. In: Vitria, J. (eds) editor Recent Advances in Artificial Intelligence Research and Development, pp. 69–76. IOS Press, (2004)

# Chapter 3
# Traffic Sign Detection

**Abstract** To detect and classify objects contained in real images, acquired in uncon-strained environments, is a challenging problem in computer vision, which complex-ity makes unfeasible the design of handcrafted solutions. In this chapter, the object detection problem is introduced, highlighting the main issues and challenges, and providing a basic introduction to the main concepts. Once the problem is formu-lated, a feature based approach is adopted for traffic sign detection, introducing the basic concepts of the machine learning framework and some bio-inspired features. Learning algorithms are explained in order to obtain good detectors using a rich description of traffic sign instances. Using the context of classical windowing detec-tion strategies, this chapter introduces an evolutionary approach to feature selection which allows building detectors using feature sets with large cardinalities.

**Keywords** Traffic sign detection · Haar-like features · Integral image · Adaboost detection · Cascade of classifiers · Evolutionary computation

The detection and classification of objects in images that have been acquired in unconstrained environments is a challenging problem, because objects can appear in different poses and lighting conditions, and against different backgrounds and clutter. This variation in object appearance makes the design of handcrafted methods for object detection impossible. Although this problem has been the subject of research since the early days of the computer vision field, it is only recently that researchers have developed generic object recognition systems for a broad class of real world objects. The breakthrough was the use of a machine learning framework that makes use of very large sets of sample images to learn robust models: Given a training set of $m$ pairs $(\rho_i, l_i)$, where $\rho_i$ is the ith image and $l_i$ is the category of the object present in $\rho_i$, the aim is to learn a model, $h(\rho_i) = l_i$ that maps images to object categories. In the specific case of traffic sign detection, $l_i \in \{-1, +1\}$, where $+1$ means presence of a traffic sign and $-1$ otherwise.

The classical methods for visual recognition involve two steps. First, a set of visual features is extracted from the image and the object of interest is represented using

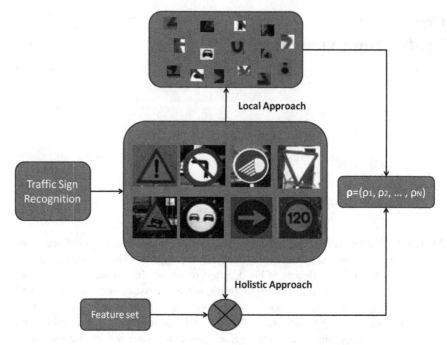

**Fig. 3.1** A representation of the two main approaches to image representation

these features. Feature selection plays a crucial role in recognition: it facilitates the identification of aspects that are shared by objects in the same class, despite the variations in their appearance, and it supports discrimination between objects and between classes that can be highly similar. In the second step a classification rule is learned from the chosen feature representation in order to recognize different instances of the object. Depending on the features extracted, a variety of classification methodologies have been proposed in the literature.

As regards the first step, there are two main approaches to deal with the feature extraction problem (see Fig. 3.1):

*Holistic methods.* use the whole object image, which corresponds to a window of the image where the object has to be detected, in order to define and extract a set of features that will represent a global view of the object. These systems are typically based on defining a template matching strategy by comparing image windows to different $m$ "templates" and recording the similarity measures in a vector. Templates can be learned from data (e.g. using Principal Component Analysis (PCA), Linear Discriminant Analysis (LDA), Non Negative Matrix Factorization (NDA) or some form of artificial neural net) or can be defined *a priori* (e.g. using a fixed wavelet dictionary or Gabor filter responses). Thus, an image $\rho_i$ can be considered to be a vector $(\rho_{i,1}, \ldots, \rho_{i,k})$ of $k$ scalar values corresponding to $k$ similarity measures.

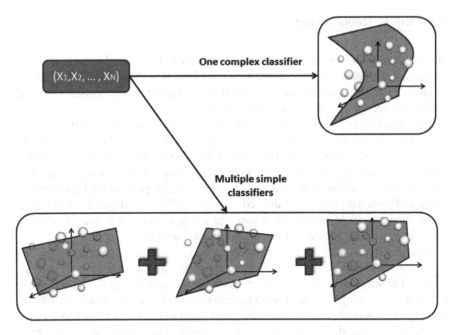

**Fig. 3.2** The two main classification approaches

*Local methods.* model an object as a collection of local visual features or "patches". Thus, an image $\rho_i$ can be considered to be a vector $(\rho_{i,1}, \ldots, \rho_{i,k})$ of $k$ patches. Each patch $\rho_{i,j}$ has a feature-vector representation $F(\rho_{i,j}) \in \Re^d$; this vector might represent various features of the appearance of a patch, as well as features of its relative location and scale. We can choose from a wide variety of features, such as UllmanĠs fragments-based representation approach [1], the gradient orientation-based SIFT [2], or some forms of geometric invariant descriptors.

As regards the second step, there are two main approaches for defining the classification rule for object representation $\rho_i$ (see Fig. 3.2): we can use a powerful $k$-dimensional classifier $h(\rho_i)$ to learn a rule for assigning the object category, or we can use a classification rule $H(\rho_i)$ based on the combination of the classification results of several "simple" classifiers $h_n(\rho_i)$. In the first case we can use the Nearest Neighbor classifier, Support/Relevance Vector Machines, neural networks, etc. In the second case, the most successful approaches have been based on different versions of the AdaBoost algorithm [3], which are based on a weighted combination of "weak" classifiers $H(\rho_i) = \sum_t \alpha_t h_t(\rho_i)$.

This chapter presents an overview of the general problem of object recognition, and introduces the basic concepts. After presenting the general scheme, we show some classical features for describing the traffic sign images, and explain a learning method for building a traffic sign detector. Finally, we introduce an evolutionary version of the learning method, which allows us to work with a larger set of features.

## 3.1 Object Recognition

Object recognition is one of the most important, but least understood, aspects of visual perception. For many biological vision systems, the recognition and classification of objects is a spontaneous, natural activity. Young children can immediately and effortlessly recognize a large variety of objects [4].

In contrast, the recognition of common objects remains way beyond the capabilities of artificial systems, or of any recognition model proposed so far. The brain generalizes spontaneously from visual examples without the need for explicit rules and laborious instruction, and is able to recognize these objects under a huge variety of viewing conditions. In contrast, computers must be programmed to recognize specific objects with fixed, well-defined shapes. It is far more difficult for an object recognition system to capture the essence of a dog, a house or a tree, the kind of classification that is natural and immediate for the human visual system.

It is not easy to define the term *object recognition* in a simple, precise and uncontroversial manner. What do we mean, exactly, when we say that we *recognize an object*? The simplest answer might be: "naming an object in sight." This answer is not entirely unambiguous, because in recognizing an object, we sometimes wish to identify an individual object or a specific *token* (such as *my car*), while in other cases recognition means identifying the object as a member of a certain class, or a type (*a truck*). We will name the first case *identification*, in which we want to identify an individual object, and the second one *classification*, in which we only want to establish the fact of belonging to a certain class.

Furthermore, an object may belong to a number of classes or categories simultaneously (e.g. my cat, a Siamese cat, a cat, an animal). In the same way, in an image we can find multiple objects, each one of which can be composed of differentiated parts. The finality of the recognition system will define the level of classification we require. In the specific case of traffic signs, we can find a classification hierarchy. For instance, a traffic sign which limits the speed to 80 km/h may be just a traffic sign, a prohibition sign, a speed limit sign, an 80 km/h limitation sign or the 80 km/h limitation sign in a certain real world position.

Object recognition is a problem that seems easy enough to overcome if we have a sufficiently large and efficient memory system. In performing recognition, we are trying to determine whether the image we are currently seeing corresponds to an object we have seen in the past. It might be possible, therefore, to approach object recognition by storing a sufficient number of different views associated with each object, and then comparing the image of the currently viewed object with all the views stored in memory [5]. Several mechanisms, known as associative memories, have been proposed for implementing this *direct* approach to recognition. A major problem with this approach is that it relies on a simple and restricted notion of similarity in order to measure the distance between the input image and each of the images previously stored in the memory. As shown in [4], the use of a simple image comparison is insufficient by itself to cope with the large variations between different images of a given object. Summarizing, for the general problem of visual object recognition this direct approach is insufficient, for two reasons: first, the space of all possible views of all the objects to be recognized is likely to be prohibitively large, and second (and more fundamentally) the image to be recognized will often not be sufficiently similar to any image seen in the past. The differences in this second case can be produced by several factors: Viewing position, photometric effects, object setting, or changing shape.

*Viewing position.* Three-dimensional objects can be viewed from a variety of viewing positions (directions and distances), and these different views can give rise to widely different images.

*Photometric effects.* These include the positions and distribution of light sources in the scene, their wavelengths, the effects of mutual illumination by other objects, and the distribution of shadows and specularities.

*Object setting.* In natural scenes, objects are rarely seen in isolation: they are usually seen against some background, next to, or partially occluded by, other objects.

*Changing shape.* Many objects, such as the human body, can maintain their identity while changing their three-dimensional shape. Changing objects, such as a pair of scissors, can sometimes be composed of rigid sub-parts. Other objects may undergo non-rigid distortions: for example, faces undergoing complex transformations due to facial expressions or hand movements.

A large variety of methods have been proposed for the task of visual object recognition, some of them as models of human vision, others as possible schemes for machine vision. Some of the proposed schemes are general in nature, while others were developed for specific application domains (see [6, 7] for reviews). In [4], Ullman classifies the basic approaches to recognition in three main classes, based on their approach to the regularity problem:

*Invariant properties methods.* Theories in this class assume that certain simple properties remain invariant under the transformations that an object is allowed to make.

*Parts decomposition methods.* Theories in this class rely on the decomposition of objects into parts. This leads to the notations of symbolic structural descriptions, feature hierarchies and syntactic pattern recognition.

*Alignment methods.* The main idea for theories in this class is to compensate for the transformations separating the viewed object and the corresponding stored model, and then to compare them.

This classification is a taxonomy of the underlying ideas, not of existing schemes. That is, a given scheme is not required to belong strictly to one of these classes, but may employ one or more of these ideas. A successful recognition scheme may in fact benefit from incorporating key ideas from all three classes.

### 3.1.1 Object Detection

Although theoretical object recognition defines the general framework for the problem faced in this chapter, we need to introduce more accurate and practical definitions to the specific case of study, i.e. the traffic sign detection problem. We use the term *object detection* to describe a specific kind of *classification*, where we have only two classes: the class *object* and the class *no object*. In this case, the class *object* corresponds to a traffic sign, while the class *no object* means that it does not contain a traffic sign.

Given an input image, the goal of object detection is to return the instances of the class *object* in this image. Therefore, object detection is often posed as a search and classification problem: a search strategy generates potential image regions and a classifier determines whether or not they are an object. The standard approach is brute-force search, in which the image is scanned in raster order using a $n \times m$ pixels window over multiple image scales. For each scale and position the window is classified. When the brute-force search strategy is used, object detection is a *rare event detection* problem, in the sense that among the millions of image regions, only a few are objects.

When facing *rare event detection* problems, we are restricted to using a fast classification strategy in order to discard those millions of windows that do not contain any object. This fact must be considered in the three main aspects of the classifier: How objects are described, how objects are modeled, and how image regions are analyzed.

## 3.2 Features

There is no universal definition of what constitutes a feature, and the exact definition often depends on the problem or the type of application. In object recognition and pattern recognition in general, the objects or phenomena being observed must be described in a computationally plausible representation. In this context, features are the individual measurable heuristic properties of the object or phenomena of interest, and are restricted by the perception of the world available, such as sensors or transaction databases. Building proper representations has become an important issue in pattern recognition [8].

In the case of computer vision, the starting point is always a matrix with numerical values which are interpreted as an image. Depending on the application, this image can represent distances from a sensor, the spectrogram of a sound or more frequently the intensity value on a light sensor matrix. Although this numerical matrix is in fact a set of features that represent the object, in general, this initial representation of the object is not enough to perform classification tasks, and more complex features must be computed. We can define a feature as any function $f : I \mapsto R$ that takes an image $I$ as input and returns a real value as output. In general, we never use a feature alone; instead, we use groups or families of features which are referred to as a feature set. While different areas of pattern recognition obviously have different features, once the features are decided they are classified by a much smaller set of algorithms. These include nearest neighbor classification in multiple dimensions, neural networks, or statistical techniques.

The description of an object by means of a set of features is known as feature extraction. Although the nature of our objects and application will suggest the features we can use, in the literature different levels of features are used for different purposes. In 1969, Levine [9] classified the features into two main groups: Microanalysis and macroanalysis. The main idea is that previous to the description of an image, we need to identify the most informative regions of that image, using a set of generalist features such as edges, lines, and so on. This initial process is called the microanalysis, while the description of the informative regions using a more problem-dependant features is called the macroanalysis. Apart from nomenclature changes (i.e. microanalysis is commonly referred to as feature detection), this division is still accepted. It is important to state that this is a fuzzy division, and some features can be classified in either of the groups depending on the application.

It seems clear, both from biological and computational evidence, that some form of data compression occurs at a very early stage in image processing. Moreover, a great deal of physiological evidence suggests that one form of this compression involves finding edges and other discriminative features in images. Edges often occur at points where there is a large variation in the luminance values in an image, and consequently they often indicate the edges, or occluding boundaries, of the objects in a scene. However, large luminance changes can also correspond to surface markings on objects. Points of tangent discontinuity in the luminance signal (rather than simple discontinuity) can also signal an object boundary in the scene.

So the first problem encountered with modeling this biological process is that of defining, precisely, what an edge might be. The usual approach is to simply define edges as step discontinuities in the image signal. Often, then, the way to localize these discontinuities is to find local maxima in the derivative of the signal, or zero-crossings in the second derivative of the signal. This idea was first suggested to the AI community, both biologically and computationally, by Marr [10], and later developed by Marr and Hildreth [11], Canny [12], and many others [13, 14].

Feature detection usually refers to the computation of points of interest where we compute the features. A point of interest is a point in the image where the local image structure around it is rich in terms of local information contents, such that the use of points of interest simplifies further processing in the vision system. In general, the points of interest are required to be invariant under local and global perturbations in the image domain, including deformations such as those arising from perspective transformations (sometimes reduced to affine transformations, scale changes, rotations and/or translations) as well as illumination/brightness variations, such that the points of interest can be computed reliably and with a high degree of reproducibility.

Once the informative regions of an object are selected, there is a long list of possible descriptors to characterize them. Most of them are based on illumination changes or on gradient information. This stage is commonly known as feature extraction. As we will see later, feature detection is sometimes mixed within the feature extraction process, and we cannot differentiate between the two processes.

### 3.2.1  Haar-Like Features

One of the most successful a priori image features, at least for a broad class of visual objects, is the Haar-like feature. Haar-like features, which are related to the discrete wavelet decomposition (DWT), were originally proposed in the framework of object detection by Viola and Jones [15] in their face detection approach.

The foundations of the DWT go back to 1976 with the studies of Croiser et al. [16] and Crochiere et al. [17], where a technique was devised in order to decompose discrete time signals. They called their analysis scheme sub-band coding, which was later improved by Vetterli and Le Gall [18] who removed the redundancy existing in the pyramidal coding scheme.

The two-dimensional Haar decomposition of a square image with $n^2$ pixels consists of $n^2$ wavelet coefficients, each of which corresponds to a distinct Haar wavelet. The first of these wavelets is the mean pixel intensity value of the whole image, and the rest of the wavelets are computed as the difference in mean intensity values of horizontally, vertically, or diagonally adjacent squares. In Fig. 3.3, a sample of a 2D decomposition of a Traffic Sign image is presented. Note that Haar wavelets are sensitive to edges in the image.

Although the Haar wavelet is widely used in the image processing and image compression fields, Haar-like features, which are a simplified version, are often used in pattern recognition. Since their appearance in the work of Viola and Jones [15] and the posterior extension in [19], Haar-like features have become a standard image feature for the detection of a broad class of visual objects. These features are based on a set of predefined patterns (see Fig. 3.4), which are defined in order to detect concrete structures in an image. Haar-like features are an extension of the Haar wavelet definition to all possible adjacent rectangles in the image.

### 3.2.2  Dissociated Dipoles

Although the representation of image structure using differential operators that compare adjacent image regions is well suited to encoding local relationships, these operators have significant drawbacks. One of the major problems arises when we try to compare distant regions of the image. In fact, any comparison of small regions across long distances is quite difficult, since an operator large enough to span the relevant distance must trade resolution for size. Alternatively, comparing distant regions by propagating information via a chain of small sized operators increases the susceptibility to the noise contributed by each of the intermediate elements.

In [20], Balas and Sinha introduce the *Dissociated Dipoles* or *Sticks operator*, for encoding non-local image relationships. These features aim to allow comparison of small images across long distances. As in the case of Haar-like features, *Dissociated Dipoles* are based on a classical wavelet image description technique, the Gabor wavelets, which have been widely applied on iris and fingerprint recognition problems.

**Fig. 3.3** Second level decomposition of a Stop Sign Image using Haar Wavelet·

While Gabor-like operators provide a simple means of representing image structure, the local image processing they embody limits a recognition system in significant ways [20]:

> Edge-based representations may fail to adapt to small changes in an image brought on by changes in object geometry or position. This particular weakness stems from more general problems with edge-based algorithms, namely that most natural images contain relatively few high-frequency (edge-like) components. Consequently, edge maps implicitly ignore most of the content of an image, and can suffer dramatically from subtle transformations that perturb edge locations while leaving large portions of the image untouched. Simple analysis also strains the capabilities of a Gabor-based representation scheme due to the conflation of the size of an operator's lobes with the distance spanned by this operator. In fact, any comparison of small regions across large distances proves quite difficult, since an operator large enough to span the relevant distance must trade resolution for size. Alternatively, comparing distant regions by propagating information via a chain of small sized operators increases susceptibility to the noise contributed by each of the intermediate elements.

Balas and Shina [20] state that the primary source of the shortcomings of the conventional differential operators is the confusion of the inter-lobe distance with

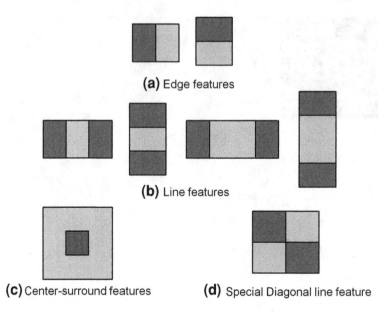

**(a)** Edge features

**(b)** Line features

**(c)** Center-surround features          **(d)** Special Diagonal line feature

**Fig. 3.4** Extended Haar-like feature patterns [19]

lobe-size. Therefore, they de-couple the lobe-size and inter-lobe distance parameters, allowing the operator to compare small regions separated by long distances. The result is the *Dissociated Dipole* or *Sticks* operator as a tool for performing non-local image comparisons.

Like a simple edge-finder, a *Dissociated Dipole* is a differential operator consisting of an excitatory and an inhibitory lobe, and may be used in any orientation or at any scale. However, unlike a conventional edge detector, the correlation of inter-lobe distance and lobe size has been removed; therefore, they allow an arbitrary separation between these two lobes. Formally, the basic form of a *Dissociated Dipole* operator comprises a pair of Gaussian lobes, each with standard deviation $\sigma$ and a spatial separation of $\delta$.

As in the case of Haar-like features, *Dissociated Dipole* has a simplified and computationally more feasible representation, introduced by Balas and Sinha in [21], in which the lobes were approximated using rectangles (see Fig. 3.5). The discrimination power of these simplified features was studied from the point of view of recognition. Note that some patterns present on Haar-like features shown in Fig. 3.4 can also be simulated with this feature set.

## 3.3  Detection Methods

Once phenomena or objects of interest have been described using the desired features, the main goal is to hypothesize their class by choosing the model that best corresponds to each sensed pattern.

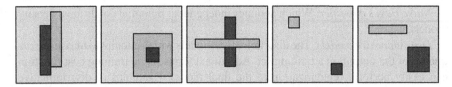

**Fig. 3.5** Examples of bilobed differential operators of the sort employed in [21]

An intriguing problem that has remained unsolved since the beginnings of pattern classification is the relationship between the structure and type of data and the performance of the different classification methodologies. In other words, it is difficult to a priori know which approach is the best for use in a given problem. Although some studies such as Van der Walt and Barnard [22] investigated very specific artificial data sets to determine conditions under which certain classifiers perform better and worse than others, the classical methodology consists of testing the performance of a set of preselected approaches and choosing the best one. This previous selection of methodologies is usually subject to problem restrictions such as dimensionality or time/complexity constraints. However, determining a suitable classifier for a given problem is still more an art than a science.

Although a wide range of classification functions exists, the first approach to a classification problem should be a linear classifier in which the classification decision is based on the value of the linear combination of the features. A linear classifier can be written as $l = h'(\rho, \mathbf{w}) = g(\mathbf{w} \cdot \rho + b)$, where $\mathbf{w}$ is a real vector of weights and $g$ is a function that converts the dot product of the two vectors into the desired output. Often $g$ is a simple function that maps all values above a certain threshold to the first class and all other values to the second class. A more complex $g$ might reflect the probability that an item belongs to a certain class $l$.

When working in a binary classification problem, one can visualize the operation of a linear classifier as splitting a high-dimensional input space with a hyperplane, where all points on one side of the hyperplane are classified as *positive*, while the others are classified as *negative*. These linear classifiers are usually referred to as *decision stumps*, and are often used in situations where the speed of classification is an issue, since they tend to be the fastest classifiers, especially when $\rho$ is sparse or has a large dimensionality. However, decision trees may be faster.

In the literature, we find two broad classes of methods for determining the parameters of a linear classifier, that is, the values of $\mathbf{w}$:

*Generative models.* Approaches that estimate $\mathbf{w}$ by modeling conditional density functions $P(\rho|\text{class})$. Examples of such algorithms include:

*Linear discriminant analysis.* (or Fisher's linear discriminant) (LDA), where Gaussian conditional density models are assumed. In spite of its name, it does not belong to the class of discriminative models in this taxonomy. However, its name makes sense when we compare LDA to the other main linear dimensionality reduction algorithm, such as Principal Components Analysis (PCA).

*Naive Bayes classifier*. Which assumes independent binomial conditional density models.

*Discriminative models*. The discriminative models which attempt to maximize the quality of the output on a training set. Additional terms in the training cost function can easily perform regularization of the final model. Examples of discriminative training of linear classifiers include

*Logistic regression*. A maximum likelihood estimation of **w** is performed assuming that the observed training set was generated by a binomial model that depends on the output of the classifier. In [23], Mitchell shows an interesting relationship between logistic regression and Naive Bayes Classifiers: The parametric form of $P(L|\rho)$ used by Logistic Regression is precisely the form implied by the assumptions of a Gaussian Naive Bayes classifier. Therefore, we can see Logistic Regression as a closely related alternative to GNB, though the two can produce different results in many cases.

*Perceptron*. An algorithm that attempts to fix all errors encountered in the training set. This is one of the most simple algorithms. Although the findings of Minsky and Papert [24] caused a significant decline in interest and funding of neural network research, and thus in the use of Perceptron, it is studied as one of the first classifiers.

*Support vector machine*. An algorithm that maximizes the margin between the decision hyperplane and the examples in the training set. SVM is considered one of the most important methods in the recent start-of-the-art in classification.

All the linear classifier algorithms listed above can be converted into non-linear algorithms operating in a different input space $\varphi(\rho)$, using the kernel trick.

Discriminative training often yields higher accuracy than modeling the conditional density functions. However, when training data is limited or when handling missing data, generative approaches may be preferable [25].

Recently, a generation of hybrid methods has been developed, combining generative models and discriminative learning in order to benefit from the two approaches. Examples of these methods can be found in [26–30].

After this general overview of detection methods, in what follows we present a general theoretical framework to machine learning to explain the AdaBoost learning algorithm, which will be used in order to deal with the traffic sign detection problem.

### 3.3.1 PAC Model of Learning

The *Probably Approximately Correct* (PAC) model of learning is a theoretical framework for studying machine learning. In this section we give only the main definitions for this model, in order to establish the basis for the study of certain learning approaches in the later sections.

**Definition 3.1** Let $\rho$ be a set called the *instance space*. We think of $\rho$ as being a set of encodings of instances or objects in the learner's world.

**Definition 3.2** A *concept* over $\rho$ is just a subset $c \subseteq \rho$ of the instance space. It can be thought of as the set of all instances that positively exemplify some simple or interesting rule. We can equivalently define a concept to be a Boolean mapping $c : \rho \to \{-1, +1\}$, with $c(\rho) = +1$ indicating that $\rho \in \rho$ is a positive example of $c$ and $c(\rho) = -1$ indicating that $\rho$ is a negative example. For this reason, $\rho$ is also called the *input space*.

A *concept class* $C$ over $\rho$ is a collection of concepts over $\rho$. Ideally, we are interested in concept classes that are sufficiently expressive for fairly general knowledge representation.

In this model, a learning algorithm will have access to positive and negative examples of an unknown *target concept* $c$, chosen from a known concept class $C$. The learning algorithm will be judged by its ability to identify a hypothesis concept that can accurately classify instances as positive or negative examples of $c$. In this model the learning algorithms "know" the target class $C$, in the sense that the designer of the learning algorithm is guaranteed that the target concept will be chosen from $C$, although he/she must design the algorithm to work for any $c \in C$.

**Definition 3.3** Let $W$ be any fixed probability distribution over the instance space $\rho$. We will refer to $W$ as the *target distribution*. If $h$ is any concept over $\rho$, then the distribution $W$ provides a natural measure of *error* between $h$ and the target concept $c$. We can define:

$$error(h) = \mathbf{Pr}_{\rho \in W}[c(\rho) \neq h(\rho)] \tag{3.1}$$

**Definition 3.4** Let $EX(c, W)$ be a procedure (sometimes called an *oracle*) that runs in unit time, and on each call returns a labeled example $\langle \rho, c(\rho) \rangle$, where $\rho$ is given randomly and independently according to $W$. A learning algorithm will have access to this procedure when learning the target concept $c \in C$. Ideally, the learning algorithm will satisfy three properties:

The number of calls to $EX(c, W)$ is small, in the sense that it is bounded by a fixed polynomial in some parameters (to be specified shortly). The amount of computation performed is small. The algorithm outputs a *hypothesis concept* $h$ such that $error(h)$ is small.

The number of calls made by a learning algorithm to $EX(c, W)$ is bounded by the running time of the learning algorithm.

Finally, the PAC model can be defined as follows:

**Definition 3.5** Let $C$ be a concept class over $\rho$. We say that $C$ is *PAC learnable* if there exists an algorithm $L$ with the following property: for every concept $c \in C$, for every distribution $W$ on $\rho$, and for all $0 < \varepsilon < 1/2$ and $0 < \delta < 1/2$, if $L$ is given access to $EX(c, W)$ and inputs $\varepsilon$ (error parameter) and $\delta$ (confidence parameter), then with probability at least $1 - \delta$, $L$ outputs a hypothesis concept $h \in C$ satisfying $error(h) \leq \varepsilon$. This probability is obtained from the random examples of $EX(c, W)$, and any internal randomization of $L$.

The hypothesis $h \in C$ of PAC learning algorithm thus has a high probability of being "approximately correct"—hence the name Probably Approximately Correct learning. For more detailed and extended definitions of the PAC model of learning, a good reference is [31].

### 3.3.2 Boosting

Learning algorithms that output only a single hypothesis suffer from three problems [32]:

*Statistical problem.* The statistical problem arises when the learning algorithm is searching a space of hypotheses that is too large for the amount of training data available. In such cases, several different hypotheses may all give the same accuracy for the training data, and the learning algorithm must choose one of these to output. There is a risk that the chosen hypothesis will not predict future data points well. When a learning algorithm suffers from this problem, it is said to have high "variance".

*Computational problem.* The computational problem arises when the learning algorithm cannot guarantee to find the best hypothesis within the hypothesis space. In some types of classifiers, such as neural networks or decision trees, the task of finding the hypothesis that best fits the training data is computationally intractable, and so heuristic methods must be employed. But these heuristics may get stuck in local minima and may fail to find the best hypothesis. When a learning algorithm suffers from this problem, it is said to have high "computational variance".

*Representation problem.* The representation problem arises when the hypothesis space does not contain any hypotheses that are good approximations to the true function $f(\rho)$. When a learning algorithm suffers from this problem, it is said to have high "bias".

All these problems can be smoothed by using a weighted vote of hypotheses. A weighted vote of equal accuracy hypotheses reduces the risk in the case of high variance methods. In the same way, considering the combination of several different local minima reduces the risk of choosing the wrong local minimum to output in methods with high computational variance. Finally, the combination of several hypotheses allows us to form a more accurate approximation to $f(\rho)$, improving the methods with high bias. A basic schema for an ensemble of classifiers that perform a weighted vote is shown in Fig. 3.6. Notice that the final hypothesis $h$ is obtained by combining classifier hypotheses $h_i$.

One of the most widely used methods to learn ensembles of classifiers is the Boosting approach, a general method for improving the accuracy of any given learning algorithm.

**Definition 3.6** Given $\varepsilon, \delta > 0$ and access to random examples, an algorithm is a *strong* PAC-learning algorithm if its output probability $1 - \delta$ has an error of at most $\varepsilon$. Further, the running time must be polynomial in $1/\varepsilon$, $1/\delta$ and other relevant parameters (namely, the "size" of the examples received, and the "size" or "complexity" of the target concept).

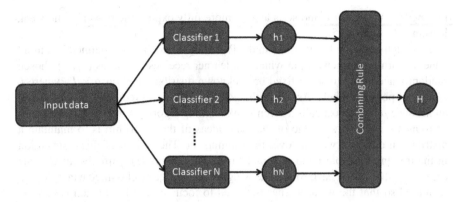

**Fig. 3.6** Ensemble of classifiers framework

**Definition 3.7** Given $\varepsilon, \delta > 0$ and access to random examples, an algorithm is a *weak* PAC-learning algorithm if its output probability $1 - \delta$ has an error of at most $\varepsilon \geq 1/2 - \gamma$, where $\gamma > 0$ is either a constant, or decreases as $1/p$ where $p$ is a polynomial in the relevant parameters [31, 33]. We will use *WeakLearn* to denote a generic weak learning algorithm.

In [34], Schapire showed that any weak learning algorithm can be efficiently transformed or "boosted" into a strong learning algorithm. Later, in [35] Freund presented the "boost-by-majority" algorithm that is considerably more efficient than Schapire's. Both algorithms work by calling a given weak learning algorithm *Weak-Learn* multiple times, each time with a different distribution over $\rho$, and finally combining all the hypotheses generated into a single hypothesis. The intuitive idea is to alter the distribution over the domain $\rho$ in a way that increases the probability of the "harder" parts of the space, thus forcing the weak learner to generate new hypotheses that make fewer mistakes in these parts.

Boost-by-majority algorithm requires that the bias $\gamma$ of the weak learning algorithm *WeakLearn* be known ahead of time, and this is an important practical deficiency. Not only is this worst-case bias usually unknown in practice, but typically the bias that can be archived by *WeakLearn* will vary considerably from one distribution to the next. Unfortunately, the boost-by-majority algorithm cannot take advantage of hypotheses computed by *WeakLearn* with an error significantly smaller than the presumed worst-case bias of $1/2 - \gamma$.

### 3.3.3 AdaBoost

In [33], Freund and Schapire introduced the Adaboost algorithm, very nearly as efficient as boost-by-majority. However, unlike boost-by-majority, the accuracy of the final hypothesis produced by Adaboost depends on the accuracy of all the hypotheses

returned by *WeakLearn*, and so is able to more fully exploit the power of the weak
learning algorithm [35].

Although boosting has its roots in the PAC model, Adaboost is defined in a more
general learning framework, in which the learner receives examples $(\rho_i, l_i)$ chosen
randomly according to some fixed but unknown distribution $P$ on $\rho \times L$, where $L$
is a set of possible labels. As usual, the goal is to learn to predict the label $l_i$ given
an instance $\rho$. Adaboost calls a given weak learning algorithm repeatedly in a series
of rounds $t = 1, \ldots, T$. One of the main ideas of the algorithm is to maintain a
distribution or set of weights over the training set. The weight of this distribution
in the training example $i$ and in round $t$ is denoted by $W_t(i)$. Initially, all weights
are set equally, but on each round, the weights of incorrectly classified examples are
increased so that the weak learner is forced to focus on the hard examples in the
training set.

The goodness of a weak hypothesis is measured by its *weighted error*

$$\varepsilon_t = Pr_{i \sim W_t}[h_t(\rho_i) \neq l_i] = \sum_{i:h_t(\rho_i) \neq l_i} W_t(i) \tag{3.2}$$

Alternatively, when the weak learner cannot be trained using the weights $W_t$ on
the training examples, a subset of the training examples can be sampled according
to $W_t$, and used to train the weak learner.

At each iteration, Adaboost calculates the updating rule $\beta_t$. The parameter $\beta_t$ is
chosen as a function of $\varepsilon_t$ and is used to update the $W_t$. The update rule reduces
the probability assigned to those examples in which the hypothesis makes a good
prediction, and increases the probability of the examples in which the prediction is
poor. Furthermore, if $h_t$ is Boolean (with range $\{0, 1\}$), then it can be shown that this
update rule exactly removes the advantage of the last hypothesis. That is, the error
of $h_t$ on distribution $W_{t+1}$ is exactly $\frac{1}{2}$. The original Adaboost algorithm proposed
by Freund and Shcapire [33] is shown in Algorithm 1.

---

**Algorithm 1** The adaptive boosting algorithm [47]

---

**Require**: A training set $\rho$ of $m$ pairs $(\rho_i, l_i)$, where $\rho_i$ is the $i^{th}$ image and
$l_i \in \{-1, +1\}$ is the category of the object present in $\rho_i$, a weak learning algorithm
(**WeakLearner**), a distribution $W$ over the $m$ examples, and the maximum number
of iterations $T$.
Initialize the weight vector: $w_i^1 = W(i) \, \forall i = 1, \ldots, m$.
**for** $t = 1, \ldots, T$ **do**
  Set

$$p^t = \frac{w^t}{\sum_{i=1}^m w_i^t}$$

  Call **WeakLearn**, providing it with the distribution $\mathbf{p}^t$: obtain a hypothesis
  $h_t: \rho \rightarrow [0, 1]$.

Calculate the error of $h_t$: $\varepsilon_t = \sum_{i=1}^{N} p_i^t |h_t(\rho_i) - h_i|$

Set $\beta_t = \frac{\varepsilon_t}{1-\varepsilon_t}$

Set the new weights vector to be

$$w_i^{t+1} = w_i^t \beta_t^{1-|h_t(\rho_i)-l_i|}$$

**end for**

**Ensure**: The final hypothesis:

$$H(\rho) = \begin{cases} 1 & \text{if } \sum_{t=1}^{T} \left(\log \frac{1}{\beta_t}\right) h_t(\rho) \geq \frac{1}{2} \sum_{t=1}^{T} \log \frac{1}{\beta_t} \\ -1 & \text{otherwise} \end{cases}$$

---

The Adaboost algorithm can be interpreted as a stagewise estimation procedure for fitting an additive logistic regression model. It optimizes an exponential criterion with the second order equivalent to the binomial log-likelihood criterion. In [36], Friedman proposes a more standard likelihood-based boosting procedure. Because this algorithm will be widely used in this thesis, we introduce a theoretical overview based on Friedman's work.

Viewing the boosting procedures as stagewise algorithms for fitting additive models helps to understand their performance. AdaBoost fits an additive model $F(\rho) = \sum_{t=1}^{T} c_t h_t(\rho)$.

We initially focus on the regression problem, where the response $l$ is quantitative, $\rho$ and $l$ have some joint distribution, and we are interested in modeling the mean $E(l|\rho) = H(\rho)$. The additive model has the form

$$H(\rho) = \sum_{j=1}^{p} f_j(\rho_j) \tag{3.3}$$

There is a separate function $f_j(\rho_j)$ for each of the $p$ input variables $\rho_j$. More generally, each component $f_j$ is a function of a small, prespecified subset of the input variables. The *backfitting algorithm* [3, 37] is a convenient modular "Gauss-Seidel" algorithm for fitting additive models. A backfitting update is

$$f_j(\rho_j) \leftarrow E\left[l - \sum_{k \neq j} f_k(\rho_k)|\rho_j\right] \quad \text{for } j = 1, 2, \ldots, p, 1, \ldots \tag{3.4}$$

Any method or algorithm for estimating a function of $f_j$ can be used to obtain an estimate of the conditional expectation in Eq. 3.4. This can include nonparametric smoothing algorithms, such as local regression or smoothing splines. On the right-hand side, all the latest versions of the functions $f_k$ are used in forming the partial residuals. The backfitting cycles are repeated until convergence. Under fairly general conditions, backfitting can be shown to converge to the minimizer of $E(l - F(\rho))^2$ [38].

Now we will consider an additive model whose elements $\{f_t(\boldsymbol{\rho})\}_1^t$ are functions of potentially all of the input features $\boldsymbol{\rho}$. In this context the $f_t(\boldsymbol{\rho})$ are taken to be simple functions characterized by a set of parameters $\gamma$ and a multiplier $\beta_t$,

$$f_t(\boldsymbol{\rho}) = \beta_t b(\boldsymbol{\rho}; \gamma_t) \tag{3.5}$$

The additive model then becomes

$$F_T(\boldsymbol{\rho}) = \sum_{t=1}^{T} \beta_t b(\boldsymbol{\rho}; \gamma_t) \tag{3.6}$$

If least-squares is used as a fitting criterion, one can solve for an optimal set of parameters through a generalized backfitting algorithm with updates

$$\{\beta_t, \gamma_t\} \leftarrow \arg\min_{\beta, \gamma} E \left[ l - \sum_{k \neq t} \beta_k b(\boldsymbol{\rho}; \gamma_k) - \beta b(\boldsymbol{\rho}; \gamma) \right]^2 \tag{3.7}$$

for $t = 1, 2, \ldots, T$ in cycles until convergence. Alternatively, one can use a "greedy" forward stepwise approach,

$$\{\beta_t, \gamma_t\} \leftarrow \arg\min_{\beta, \gamma} E \left[ l - F_{t-1}(\boldsymbol{\rho}) - \beta b(\boldsymbol{\rho}; \gamma) \right]^2 \tag{3.8}$$

for $t = 1, 2, \ldots, T$ where $\{\beta_k, \gamma_k\}_i^{t-1}$ are fixed at their corresponding solution values at earlier iterations.

In boosting jargon, $f(\boldsymbol{\rho}) = \beta b(\boldsymbol{\rho}; \gamma)$ would be called a *weak learner* and $F_T(\boldsymbol{\rho})$ (Eq. 3.6) the *committee*. At this point note that the backfitting procedure, independently of the version we use (the general or the greedy) only requires an algorithm for fitting a *single* weak learner Eq. 3.5 to data. This base algorithm is simply applied repeatedly to modified versions of the original data

$$h_t \leftarrow l - \sum_{k \neq t} f_k(\boldsymbol{\rho}) \tag{3.9}$$

In the forward stepwise procedure (Eq. 3.8), the modified output $h_t$ at the $t$th iteration depends only on its value $h_{t-1}$ and the solution $h_{t-1}(\boldsymbol{\rho})$ at the previous iteration,

$$l_m = l_{m-1} - f_{m-1}(\boldsymbol{\rho}) \tag{3.10}$$

At each step $t$, the previous output value $l_{t-1}$ is modified so that the previous model $f_{t-1}$ has no explanatory power on the new outputs $l_t$. One can therefore view this as a procedure for boosting a weak learner $f(\boldsymbol{\rho}) = \beta b(\boldsymbol{\rho}; \gamma)$ to form a powerful committee $F_M(\boldsymbol{\rho})$.

Now, consider minimizing the criterion:

$$J(F) = E\left(e^{-yF(\rho)}\right) \tag{3.11}$$

for estimation of $F(\rho)$. Here $E$ represents expectation: depending on the context, this may be a population expectation (with respect to a probability distribution) or else a sample average. $E_w$ indicates a weighted expectation. Lemma 1 shows that the function $F(\rho)$ that minimizes $J(F)$ is the symmetric logistic transform of $P(l = 1|\rho)$. (The proof can be found in [36]).

**Lemma 1** *$E(e^{-yF(\rho)})$ is minimized at*

$$F(\rho) = \frac{1}{2} \log \frac{P(l = 1|\rho)}{P(l = -1|\rho)} \tag{3.12}$$

*Hence*

$$P(l = 1|\rho) = \frac{e^{F}(\rho)}{e^{-F(\rho)} + e^{F(\rho)}} \tag{3.13}$$

$$P(l = -1|\rho) = \frac{e^{-F(\rho)}}{e^{-F(\rho)} + e^{F(\rho)}} \tag{3.14}$$

**Corollary 2** *If E is replaced by averages over regions of $\rho$ where $F(\rho)$ is constant (as in the terminal node of a decision tree), the same result applies to the sample proportions*

**Result 3** The Discrete Adaboost algorithm builds an additive logistic regression model via Newton-like updates for minimizing $E(e^{-yF(\rho)})$.

### 3.3.3.1 Adaboost Variants

Since Freund and Schapire presented their AdaBoost algorithm, many other versions of this algorithm have been developed. All these versions differ in the manner in which they modify the weights and construct the final hypothesis. In the following sections we show the algorithms for some of these versions. Like the original AdaBoost algorithm, all their versions can be interpreted from a statistical point of view [36]. In what follows, the key points and algorithms of some different versions are introduced. Notice that the versions differ slightly in the way they update the weights and in the output formulation.

*Real Adaboost.* The *Real AdaBoost* algorithm builds an additive logistic regression by stagewise and approximate optimization of $J(F) = E\left[e^{-lF(\rho)}\right]$. The Real Adaboost can be viewed as an Adaboost with Confidence Weighted Predictions, in the sense that it uses class probability estimates $p_t(\rho)$ to construct real-valued contributions $f_t(\rho)$. The algorithm is shown in Algorithm 2.

---

**Algorithm 2** The Real AdaBoost Algorithm

---

**Require**: A training set $\rho$ of $m$ pairs $(\rho_i, l_i)$, where $\rho_i$ is the $i^{\text{th}}$ image and $l_i \in \{-1, +1\}$ is the category of the object present in $\rho_i$, a weak learning algorithm (**WeakLearner**) and the maximum number of iterations $T$.
Initialize the weight vector $w_i = \frac{1}{m}, i = 1, 2, \ldots, m$
**for** $t = 1, \ldots, T$ **do**
  Use the WeakLearn in order to fit the classifier to obtain a class probability estimate $p_t(\rho) = \hat{P}_w(l = 1|\rho) \in [-1, 1]$, using weights $w_i$ on the training data
  Set $f_t(\rho) \leftarrow \frac{1}{2} \log \frac{p_t(\rho)}{1 - p_t(\rho)} \in \mathbf{R}$
  Set $w_i \leftarrow w_i e^{-l_i f_t(\rho_i)}, i = 1, 2, \ldots, m$, and renormalize so that $\sum_i w_i = 1$.
**end for**
**Ensure**: The final hypothesis:

$$F_T = sign\left(\sum_{t=1}^{T} f_t(\rho)\right)$$

---

*LogitAdaboost*. The *LogitAdaboost* algorithm uses Newton steps for fitting an additive symmetric logistic model by maximum likelihood. The algorithm is shown in Algorithm 3.

---

**Algorithm 3** The Logit AdaBoost Algorithm

---

**Require**: A training set $\rho$ of $m$ pairs $(\rho_i, l_i)$, where $\rho_i$ is the $i^{\text{th}}$ image and $l_i \in \{-1, 1\}$ is the category of the object present in $\rho_i$, a weak learning algorithm (**WeakLearner**) and the maximum number of iterations $T$.
Start with weights $w_i = \frac{1}{m}, i = 1, 2, \ldots, m$, $F(\rho) = 0$ and probability estimates $p(\rho_i) = \frac{1}{2}$
**for** $t = 1, \ldots, T$ **do**
  Compute the working response

$$z_i = \frac{h_i^* - p(\rho_i)}{p(\rho_i)(1 - p(\rho_i))}$$

  where $h_i^*$ represents outcome and is a $-1/+1$ response.
  Compute the weights

$$w_i = p(\rho_i)(1 - p(\rho_i))$$

  Find the function $f_t(\rho)$ by a weighted least-squares regression of $z_i$ to $\rho_i$ using weights $w_i$.
  Update $F(\rho) \leftarrow F(\rho) + \frac{1}{2} f_t(\rho)$ and $p(\rho) \leftarrow \frac{e^{F(\rho)}}{e^{F(\rho)} + e^{-F(\rho)}}$
**end for**

**Ensure**: The final hypothesis:

$$F_T = sign[F(\rho)] = sign \left[ \sum_{t=1}^{T} f_t(\rho) \right]$$

*Gentle Adaboost.* The *Gentle Adaboost* algorithm uses Newton steps for mini-mizing $E \left[ e^{-yF(\rho)} \right]$. This is a modified version of the *Real Adaboost*, using Newton stepping rather than exact optimization at each step. The algorithm is shown in Algorithm 4.

---

**Algorithm 4** The Gentle AdaBoost Algorithm

---

**Require**: A training set $\rho$ of $m$ pairs $(\rho_i, l_i)$, where $\rho_i$ is the $i^{\text{th}}$ image and $l_i \in \{-1, 1\}$ is the category of the object present in $\rho_i$, a weak learning algorithm (**WeakLearner**) and the maximum number of iterations $T$.

Initialize the weight vector $w_i = \frac{1}{m}, i = 1, 2, \ldots, m$

Initialize $F(\rho) = 0$

**for** $t = 1, \ldots, T$ **do**

    Fit the regression function $f_t$ by weighted least-squares of $l_i$ to $\rho_i$ with weights $w_i$.

    Update $F(\rho) \leftarrow F(\rho) + f_t(\rho)$

    Update $w_i \leftarrow w_i e^{-l_i f_t(\rho_i)}$ and renormalize.

**end for**

**Ensure**: The final hypothesis:

$$F_T = sign[F(\rho)] = sign \left[ \sum_{t=1}^{T} f_t(\rho) \right]$$

---

In addition to the Adaboost variants that differ according to their use of the error values to update the weights, in the literature we can find different modifications in order to improve other aspects of the obtained classifiers. For instance, Mita [39] improves the generalization performance by using weak classifiers that include multiple features simultaneously. Feature co-occurrence makes it possible to classify difficult samples that are misclassified by weak classifiers using a single feature.

## 3.4 Evolutionary Approach

Rectangular features are rather primitive when compared with alternatives such as steerable filters [40]. Steerable filters, and their relatives, are excellent for the detailed analysis of boundaries, image compression, and texture analysis. In contrast, rectangle features, while sensitive to the presence of edges, bars and other simple image structures, are quite coarse. Unlike steerable filters, only a few orientations of the rectangle features are possible.

In spite of their simplicity, rectangular features provide a rich image representation which supports effective learning. Their extreme computational efficiency provides ample compensation for their limited flexibility. Rectangular features have the property that a single feature can be evaluated at any scale and location in a few operations.

It is important to note that Haar features constitute an overcomplete dictionary of the image and that there are more than $2^{18}$ different features for a small image window of 576 pixels ($24 \times 24$ pixels). This fact imposes a high computational cost on the learning step of the Adaboost algorithm, which involves several rounds of exhaustive searches. From a practical point of view, when using conventional hardware the development of a high performance object detector represents a learning time of the order of several hundred hours.

The work of Viola and Jones [15] was expanded on by Lienhart and Maydt [19], who showed that the use of a larger feature set may improve the convergence and performance of the final classifier. The extension of the feature set was done by adding rotated versions of original Haar-like features, and thus adding a factor to the exponential relation between the size of the feature set and the training time. In order to allow the use of extended feature sets, a redefinition of the classical approach is needed in order to avoid an exhaustive search over the feature space. In what follows, we introduce the evolutionary computation, and redefine the classical approach to take advantage of evolutionary methods that allow us to work with huge feature sets.

### 3.4.1 Introduction

Darwin hypothesized that living beings adapted and differentiated to varying conditions or niches in their environment through a process of evolution. Although in DarwinĠs times genetics was an unknown field, most of the studies which are based on evolution assume current knowledge on genetics and define algorithms based on chromosome-based encoding and the processes observed in the natural evolution of species. However, the Darwinian processes can be defined in a more general manner, with no assumptions about the implementation of these processes. This more general definition has been widely developed in memetics [41, 42], the field that attempts to cope with evolutionary models of information transmission. These models have been used to represent certain brain functions and social conducts. In [42], Calvin defines the essential processes in any evolutionary model, in order to ensure quality improvement over generations:

1. There must be a pattern involved.
2. The pattern must be copied somehow.
3. Variant patterns must sometimes be produced by chance.
4. The pattern and its variant must compete with one another for occupation of a limited work space.

5. The competition is biased by a multifaceted environment. This is Darwin's natural selection.
6. New variants always preferentially occur around the more successful of the current patterns. This is what Darwin later called an inheritance principle.

In addition to these essential processes, Calvin [42] introduced five other processes which can notably influence the rate of evolutionary change:

1. Stability may occur. Variants happen, but they are either nonviable or backslide easily.
2. Systematic recombination (crossing over, sex) generates many more variants than do copying errors and the far-rarer point mutations.
3. Fluctuating environments, shaping up more complex patterns capable of doing well in several environments.
4. Parcellation typically speeds evolution. It raises the surface-to-volume ratio (or perimeter-to-area ratio) and exposes a higher percentage of the population to the marginal conditions on the margins.
5. Local extinctions speed evolution because they create empty niches.

After introducing Darwinian processes, Calvin [43] defines a *Darwin machine* by analogy to a Turing machine, as a machine that involves an iteration process that yields a high-quality result. However, whereas a Turing machine uses logic, the Darwin machine uses rounds of variation, selection, and inheritance. In its original connotation, a *Darwin machine* is any process that bootstraps quality by utilizing all of the six essential features of a Darwinian process: A pattern is copied with variations, where populations of one variant pattern compete with another population, their relative success being biased by a multifaceted environment so that winners predominate in producing the further variants of the next generation.

The theoretical definition of a *Darwin machine* states the necessary conditions for evolution. There are various possibilities for implementing these processes. The most widely applied implementation aims to copy the natural implementation of those processes, using genetic theories, and is what we refer to as *Genetic Darwin Machine*. Another possibility is to use probabilistic models in order to implement these processes. Although in the literature these methods can be found under a wide set of different names, we group them together under the name of *Probabilistic Darwin Machines*. We first define the basic concepts for both implementations and the following sections analyze in depth some examples of implementation for both families of *Darwin machines*. Figure 3.7 shows a graphic comparison between the theoretical Darwin Machine and the Genetic Darwin Machine.

### 3.4.1.1 Genetic Darwin Machine

All living organisms are *coded* by means of their genetic material, represented in DNA chains. The DNA contains all the information used in the development and functioning of all known living organisms and some viruses. Within cells, DNA is

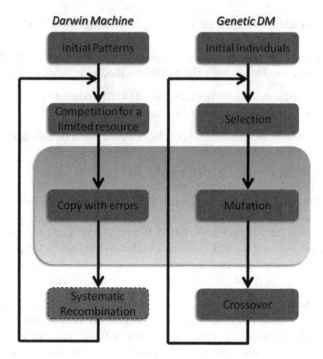

**Fig. 3.7** Graphic comparison between Darwin Machines and Genetic Darwin Machines. Although systematic recombination is an optional operation in Darwin Machines, it is usually implemented by Genetic Darwin Machines

organized into structures called chromosomes, and the set of all the chromosomes is called the genome.

The genetic information is used as a recipe to create other structures of the cells such as proteins, which are responsible of most part of the processes of the organism, and therefore, the way in which the genetic information is expressed. Therefore, the capabilities and characteristics of an organism, and thus their ability to adapt to the environment, depend on the information contained in the chromosomes. Evolution concerns the natural processes that allow the perpetuation of useful genetic information and its improvement in order to adapt to changes in the environment.

The basis of any evolutionary algorithm relies on the concept of *Natural Selection*, in which the best individuals can survive and reproduce in order to perpetuate their species. The genetic information of those best individuals is transferred over generations, obtaining better individuals and improving the species. In general, in natural evolution, individuals are classified by their adaptation level: the best individuals are the ones that are most adapted to the environment. Apart from this information pathway through the generations, there are two other sources of evolution:

*Crossover.* In the reproduction process, two individuals of a population interchange their genetic information. Thus, the offspring have a genetic information that contains parts of both their parents. When this mixing leads to a better adaptation to the environment, the new individuals will survive and this new genetic information will persist generation after generation. In the opposite case, if that the offspring do not survive, the new information will be discarded.

*Mutation.* In contrast to crossover, in which existing information is combined, in the case of mutation, new information can be generated. Mutation consists of randomly changing small parts of the genetic information. Analogously to crossover, when these changes imply better adaptation, they will be passed down the generations. Mutation allows evolution to generate new species.

Darwin explains the evolution of species from the inference of these processes (selection and variability), and the subsequent advances in our knowledge of genetics has defined how these aspects are accomplished by all living beings in nature. Biological evidence of the implementation of those concepts in nature is used in order to simulate natural evolution in a computational manner.

One of the first computational approaches to natural evolution was presented by Nils A. Barricelli [44], one of the pioneers in evolutionary computation. His initial experiments comprised a simple simulation of numbers in a grid. The numbers moved in the grid according to local rules that were specified for each number [45]. Barricelli made several observations about the patterns that emerged from such simple rules, which he termed *organisms*. Organisms were defined to be independent if they could reproduce without requiring other organisms of a different pattern, which he termed *another species*. He noted patterns of recombination, including a multiple point operation in which two patterns would collide and the result would be a new self-sustaining pattern with numbers chosen from each of the *parents*. Overall, Barricelli's search for emergent patterns is reminiscent of the search for emergent properties in complex adaptive systems that pervaded artificial life research in the late 1980s and early 1990s.

Beginning in 1957 with the work [46], the Australian quantitative geneticist Alex Fraser published a series of papers addressing different aspects from basic concepts to specific topics such as the simulation of artificial selection of organisms with multiple loci (position of a gene in the genome) controlling a measurable trait [47]. These initial studies established the basis of evolutionary computation. In the early 1960s computer simulation of evolution by biologists became more common and the methods were described in books by Fraser and Burnell [48], Crosby [49], and the Ph.D thesis by Rechenberg [50], which provided a comprehensive overview of the work carried out over a decade. Fraser's simulations included all the essential elements of the most widely used and probably most known *Genetic Darwin Machine*, the *Genetic Algorithms*, but they did not become popular until the publication of applied studies such as Schwefel [51], which used evolutionary computationto solve engineering problems.

Since the popularization of evolutionary algorithms, they have been widely used in several optimization problems, such as scheduling and function minimization. The fundamental approach to optimization is to formulate a single standard of measurement (a cost function) that summarizes the performance or value of a decision and iteratively improves this performance by selecting from among the available alternatives. The cost function or evaluation function is the measure of adaptation of a certain *organism* (solution) to the environment (problem). An in-depth study of the definition and implementation of *Genetic Algorithms* is presented in Sect. 3.4.4. Note that some strategies commonly used in *Genetic Algorithms*, such as crossover and parallel evolutions are described in the general model as non-essentials.

### 3.4.2 From Object Detection to Function Optimization

The combination of Genetic Darwin Machines and AdaBoost has been exploited by various authors in recent years. Sedai and Rhee [52] proposed the use of Genetic Algorithms to create subsets of features which adapt better to certain classification tasks and combine specific subsets using AdaBoost. Treptow et al. [53] uses a Genetic Algorithm in order to evolve an extension of the Haar-like features, using AdaBoost to combine the evolved features.

We now explain how the process of learning a detector can be approached as a function optimization problem, using Genetic Darwin Machines for implementation.

Given a training set $\langle (\boldsymbol{\rho}_1, l_1), \ldots, (\boldsymbol{\rho}_m, l_m) \rangle$, where $l_i \in \{-1, +1\}$ is the target value for sample $\boldsymbol{\rho}_i$, the goal of an object detection learning algorithm is to deal with the inference of a strong classifier $H(\boldsymbol{\rho}_i) = l_i$. In the boosting framework, we define a distribution $W = \{w_1, \ldots, w_m\}$ over the training set, where each $w_i$ is the weight associated to the sample $\boldsymbol{\rho}_i$, and $H(\boldsymbol{\rho})$ corresponds to an additive model $H(\boldsymbol{\rho}) = \sum_t \alpha_t h_t(\boldsymbol{\rho})$ where the final decision is a combination of the decisions of several *weak classifiers* $h(\boldsymbol{\rho}) \in \{-1, +1\}$. In contrast to the strong classifier $H(\boldsymbol{\rho})$ where we expect a good performance for any sample $\boldsymbol{\rho}_i$ in the training set, in the case of weak classifier we only expect it to be better than a random decision.

Given $\mathcal{H}$ the set of all possible weak classifiers, $h^s \in \mathcal{H}$ a certain weak classifier defined by parameters $\mathbf{s}$, $W$ the weight distribution of the Adaboost and $\varepsilon(h^s) = Pr_{i \sim W}[h^s(\boldsymbol{\rho}_i) \neq l_i]$ the error function, the regression step consists in finding $\mathbf{s}^*$ that $\varepsilon(h^{s^*}) \leq \varepsilon(h^s) | \forall h^{s^*}, h^s \in \mathcal{H}$, where the complexity of finding $\mathbf{s}^*$ depends on the size of $\mathcal{H}$. In Algorithm 5, the evolutionary version for the Discrete Adaboost is shown. Note that the only difference vis-à-vis the classical Discrete AdaBoost is the way in which the weak hypothesis $h_t$ is obtained. The same approach can be used in all the variants of AdaBoost.

---

**Algorithm 5** Evolutionary Discrete Adaboost

---

**Require**: A training set $\boldsymbol{\rho}$ of $m$ pairs $(\boldsymbol{\rho}_i, l_i)$, where $\boldsymbol{\rho}_i$ is the $i^{\text{th}}$ image and $l_i \in \{-1, +1\}$ is the category of the object present in $\boldsymbol{\rho}_i$, an evolutionary weak learning algorithm (**EvolWeakLearner**) and the maximum number of iterations $M$.

    **Initialize** the weight vector: $w_i^1 = \frac{1}{m}$ for $i = 1, \ldots, m$.

    for $t = 1, \ldots, m$ **do**

        Set

$$p^t = \frac{w^t}{\sum_{i=1}^{m} w_i^t}$$

Call the evolutionary method **EvolWeakLearner**, providing it with the distribution $\mathbf{p}^t$. Obtain a hypothesis $h_t : \rho \rightarrow \{-1, +1\}$. which minimizes:

$$\varepsilon_t = Pr_{i \sim W_t}[h_t(\rho_i) \neq l_i]$$

Obtain weak hypothesis $h_t(\rho) \mapsto \{-1, +1\}$ with error $\varepsilon_t$
Update:

$$W_{t+1}(i) \leftarrow W_t(i) \times \exp(-l_i \times h_t(\rho_i))$$

Normalize $W_{t+1}$ so

$$\sum_{i=1}^{m} W_{t+1}(i) = 1$$

**end for**
**Ensure**: the final hypothesis:

$$H(\rho) = sign\left(\sum_{t=1}^{T} h_t(\rho)\right)$$

---

Once the evolutionary approach is defined, in order to detect an object we need to define $\mathbf{s}$. In general terms, $\mathbf{s}$ is the set of all the parameters that defines a *weak hypothesis*, and therefore, it is closely related to the features we use to describe the objects and how decisions are made. We can divide $\mathbf{s} = \{s_1, \ldots, s_D\}$ into two different subsets $\mathbf{s}_M = \{s_1, \ldots, s_i\}$ and $\mathbf{s}_F = \{s_{i+1}, \ldots, s_D\}$, which contain the parameters of the decision method and the parameters of the features respectively.

*Features parametrization.* The first step in object detection is to choose a description method for the images. No restrictions on the type of features are assumed, and so any of the features introduced in Sect. 3.2 or any other descriptors we can imagine can be used to describe objects. In general, certain feature-specific parameters must be defined in order to use each descriptor (i.e. regions of a Haar-like feature or Dissociated Dipole, number of bins in the SIFT and SURF descriptors, etc.). These parameters can be discrete or continuous, predefined or learned, etc. All these parameters are included in $\mathbf{s}_F$. Given an instance for each parameters, we must be able to represent an object, using either a single value (i.e. Haar-like) or a vector (i.e. SIFT).

*Classifier parametrization.* Once the object is described, a decision must be performed using the descriptor associated to the object. Although there are different approaches for generating hypotheses from descriptors, in general we can consider threshold based decisions when objects are described by a single value, and some type of distance metric. In the first case, the threshold value and the polarity value must be included as parameters. In the second case, parameters to define the metric or reference points can be added on the parameters. Moreover, once the distance is evaluated, the decision should be generated using a threshold like approach, and thus, the threshold and polarity parameters will also be included as classifier parameters $s_M$.

### 3.4.3  Evolutionary Object Detection Approach

At this point, the object detection approach based on a boosting strategy has been redefined as the problem of finding the parameters $s$ that minimize the weighted error function $\varepsilon(h^s)$, that is, an optimization problem. The classical approaches perform an exhaustive search over the parameter space in order to find the best values. Although this can be done when the number of values that parameters can take is reduced, it is impossible in large search spaces.

In the literature we find many different approaches to dealing with optimization problems with large search spaces, most of them based on gradient descent, such as line search methods, normalized steepest methods or the Newton steps method. In these methods, the goal function must be differentiable, and uses the gradient direction to move from a certain solution to a better one. In general, this restriction cannot be guaranteed for the error function, where small changes in the parameters can produce large discontinuities in the error function. In this scenario, the most common optimization methodologies are based on evolutionary computation; in general, the first choice are Genetic Algorithms.

Once a general formulation and its considerations are provided, the first step is to check that using evolutionary strategies we can obtain the same results as in the case of exhaustive methods. Therefore, we need to define a framework in which both approaches can be applied, and compare their learning capabilities. Below we define a parametrization for Haar-like features using decision stumps, analogously to the approach of Viola and Jones.

#### 3.4.3.1  Classifier Implementation

In order to predict the classifier value of a certain object, a decision stump will be used in all the experiments. As we saw in Sect. 3.3, the decision stump is a linear classifier that uses a hyperplane to classify points in a binary problem. The parameters related to a decision stump are hyperplane parameters that codify how the space is divided (see Fig. 3.8) and a polarity value which decides which class is on each side of the hyperplane (see Fig. 3.9).

Given an object descriptor $\mathbf{d} \in R^N$, classifier parameters can be defined as $s_M = \{s_p \in \{-1, +1\}, \mathbf{s}_h \in R^N\}$, where $s_p$ is the polarity value and $\mathbf{s}_h$ the parameters of the hyperplane.

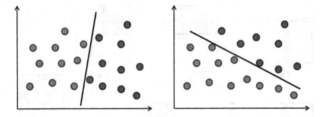

**Fig. 3.8** Two different instances of the hyperplane parameters. There are an infinity of possible instances for the hyperplane parameters

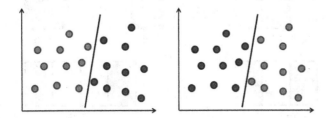

**Fig. 3.9** The polarity value codifies which side of the hyperplane corresponds to each class. There are only two possible values for this parameter

### 3.4.3.2 Features Implementation

Object description will be performed using the Haar-like features used in the work of Viola and Jones (see Sect. 3.2.1). Given the region configuration, a feature is determined with only one of its regions. Figure 3.10 presents the different configurations considered.

Therefore, codifying a Haar-like feature is equivalent to codifying just one rectangle and the configuration. A rectangle can be easily computed by codifying its upper-left corner and its vertical and horizontal sizes (see Fig. 3.11).

Moreover, an additional parameter $s_f$ can be added in order to flip between excitatory and inhibitory regions, obtaining complementary features (excitatory regions become inhibitory and viceversa). Using all the above definitions, the parametrization for a Haar-like feature can be written as $s_F = \{s_x, s_y, s_w, s_h, s_t, s_f\}$, where $s_x, s_y, s_w, s_h \in N$, $s_t \in \{1, \ldots, 8\}$, and $s_f \in \{-1, 1\}$.

### 3.4.3.3 Final Model

Once all the parameters involved in the weak hypothesis have been described, we can define the parameter vector $s = s_M \cup s_F = \{s_p, s_h, s_x, s_y, s_w, s_h, s_t, s_f\}$. Since Haar-like features describe an image with a single value, $s_h$ has dimension one and corresponds to a threshold value. Although all these parameters must be optimized in order to obtain a good weak hypothesis, not all of them have to be learned using

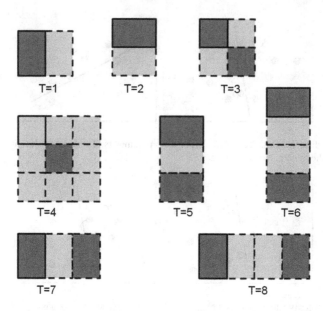

**Fig. 3.10** Different Haar-like region configurations. Dashed lines correspond to regions inferred from the given region, which are represented with a continuous line. Darker regions correspond to inhibitory (negative) regions while lighter ones are the excitatory (positive) regions

**Fig. 3.11** Parametrization of a region in an image

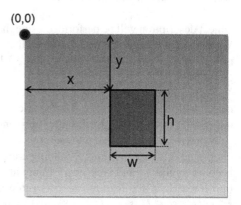

an evolutionary approach: some of them can either be learned using other methods or fixed to a certain value. For instance, the threshold value of the classifier can be exhaustively found once the feature parameters have been learned with an evolutionary approach.

At this point, a simplification respect to the Viola and Jones approach is applied to our method. The simplification is to use threshold value fixed to zero, known in the literature as Òordinal featuresÓ. This term is related to the use of the sign instead of the value of the feature. In [54], a face detection approach is presented using only the sign of region intensity differences. The authors demonstrate that by removing the magnitude of the difference the model becomes more stable to illumination changes and image degradation. With this approach, we can remove the threshold value from the parameter vector. Moreover, using ordinal features, it is easy to verify that $s_p$ and $s_f$ have the same effect on the classification value, and therefore, only one of them need be learnt.

Finally, using all above considerations, the problem consists in finding the model parameters:

$$\mathbf{s} = \{s_p, s_x, s_y, s_w, s_h, s_t\} \tag{3.15}$$

which minimize the weighted error function of the AdaBoost, under the following constraints:

$$\begin{aligned}
s_p &\in \{-1, 1\} \\
s_x, s_y &\geq 0 \\
s_w, s_h &> 0 \\
s_x + s_w &< W \\
s_y + s_h &< H \\
s_t &\in \{1, \ldots, 8\}
\end{aligned} \tag{3.16}$$

where $W$ and $H$ corresponds to the width and height of the learning window.

### 3.4.4 Object Detection Based on Genetic Algorithms

Now we have formulated the problem, in this section we present the implementation of an evolutionary weak learner based on Genetic Algorithms. The first step is to define a chromosome-based representation for problem variables in Eq. 3.15. Once the encoding is discussed, the adaptation of a certain individual restricted to the constraints in Eq. 3.15 must be included in the evaluation function. Finally, we present an experiment to verify if the resulting schema is able to learn.

#### 3.4.4.1 Chromosome Encoding

Although the encoding of a problem in a chromosome-like representation can be performed in multiple ways, the use of binary representation simplifies mutation and cross-over operators, and it is the method recommended in most problems. Since all our variables are integers, their representation do not need to store decimal positions. In addition, the ranges for each variable are known, and so we can adjust the number of bits in order to minimize values outside the valid ranges.

As a general rule, the number of bits needed to represent a parameter $x$ which take values inside a range [MinVal, ..., MaxVal], can be calculated as:

**Table 3.1** Number of bits to represent each parameter

| Parameter name | Initial range | Final range | Number of bits |
|---|---|---|---|
| $s_p$ | $\{-1, +1\}$ | $[0_{-1}, 1_{+1}]$ | 1 |
| $s_x$ | $[0, W - 1]$ | $[0, W - 1]$ | $\lceil \log_2 W \rceil$ |
| $s_y$ | $[0, H - 1]$ | $[0, H - 1]$ | $\lceil \log_2 H \rceil$ |
| $s_w$ | $[0, W - 1]$ | $[0, W - 1]$ | $\lceil \log_2 W \rceil$ |
| $s_h$ | $[0, H - 1]$ | $[0, H - 1]$ | $\lceil \log_2 H \rceil$ |
| $s_t$ | $[1, 8]$ | $[0, 7]$ | 3 |

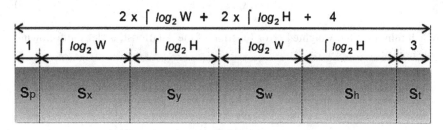

**Fig. 3.12** Final chromosome representation for an ordinal Haar-like feature based weak learner. The number of bits is calculated over a learning window of $W \times H$ pixels

$$\text{NumBits} = \lceil \log_2 (\text{MaxValue} - \text{MinValue} + 1) \rceil \qquad (3.17)$$

in the case of variables that take values from a set of non-contiguous values, we need to define a range of continuous values and map each value from the original value set to one of the values in the contiguous range defined.

In order to codify the parameter, we need to move it from its original range to a zero based range $\{0, \ldots, \text{MaxVal} - \text{MinVal}\}$ and codify the resulting number in a binary representation. Analogously, when we need to recover the value of a certain parameter, we need to decode the value codified in a binary format to its decimal representation and move this value to its original range.

Using the representation above, we need to differentiate between the parameters which depend on the problem (and for which we therefore need problem information to decode) and those that are independent. Basically, the only problem information we need is the size of the training window, in order to adjust the range of region parameters (see Fig. 3.11). Assuming a training window of $W \times H$ pixels, the ranges and number of bits needed to represent each parameter is shown in Table 3.1.

The final chromosome representation for an individual is shown in Fig. 3.12, where the width of each field in bits and the final number of bits is represented. The last consideration in order to obtain the final representation is how we codify a decimal number to its binary representation. We adopt a codification in terms of Gray codes, which guarantee that similar representations correspond to similar values, although a direct binary representation could be used instead.

### 3.4.4.2 Evaluation Function

The goal of the evaluation function is to assign an adaptation value to each chromosome. The first step is to decode the chromosome into the original parameter vector, and to evaluate whether those parameters fulfill the constraints or not. When one individual does not fulfill some of the problem constrains, we have two possibilities:

*Fixed Error Value.* Since we are working on a minimization problem, we can define a value greater than the worst possible value that an individual can achieve. Therefore, in the evolutionary process, the individual will have near null possibilities to be selected for next generations.

*Informative Error Value.* The idea is similar to the fixed error value approach, but in this case, instead of returning a fixed value, we calculate a value according to how near the individual is to fulfilling the constraints. Therefore, if in some generation of the evolutionary process a large number of bad individuals is present, it is possible to evolve to a good individual. If a fixed value is used, no difference between bad individuals is provided, making evolution to a good individual impossible.

Since in our case the range is adjusted to the possible values, we are more likely to have a large amount of valid individuals, and a fixed error value is used in order to obtain a faster evaluation function.

For valid individuals, the weighted error function is calculated using a training set and the weights associated to each sample. This process is summarized in Algorithm 6. Note that a function $f_s$ must be defined, which calculates the value of the Haar-like feature. This process can be done using an image representation based on integral images [15]. In this implementation, the polarity value $s_p$ is the classifier polarity, therefore, $f_s$ does not consider a polarity value and it is applied over the final hypothesis. Note also that a fixed error value of 1.1 is used to indicate when the individual does not fulfill the constraints. Since the worst possible error value is 1.0, this assigned value is assumed to be always worse than the maximum error value for a valid classifier.

---

**Algorithm 6** Evaluation function for ordinal Haar-like feature chromosome based representation.

---

**Require**: A training set $X$ of $N$ pairs $(\mathbf{x}_i, y_i)$, where $\mathbf{x}_i$ is the $i^{th}$ image and $y_i \in \{-1, 1\}$ is the category of the object present in $\mathbf{x}_i$, a weight distribution $W = \{w_1, \ldots, w_N\}$ where $w_i$ is the weight of $i^{th}$ sample in $X$, the chromosome $C$ to be evaluated, and $f_s(x) \mapsto Z$ which calculates the value of the Haar-like feature parameterized in $\mathbf{s} = \{s_x, s_y, s_w, s_h, s_t\}$ over a given image $\mathbf{x}$.

Decode the chromosome $C$ into the parameter vector $\mathbf{s} = \{s_p, s_x, s_y, s_w, s_h, s_t\}$.

**if** $\mathbf{s}$ fulfill the constraints of the problem **then**

    Initialize $\varepsilon \leftarrow 0$

    **for** $i = 1, \ldots, N$ **do**

        **if** $f_s(x_i) \geq 0$ **then**

            $h_i \leftarrow +1$

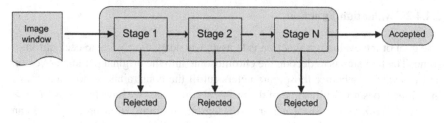

**Fig. 3.13** The attentional cascade

>           **else**
>               $h_i \leftarrow -1$
>           **end if**
>           $h_i \leftarrow h_i \times s_p$
>           **if** $h_i \neq y_i$ **then**
>               $\varepsilon \leftarrow \varepsilon + w_i$
>           **end if**
>       **end for**
>   **else**
>       $\varepsilon \leftarrow 1.1$
>   **end if**
> **Ensure**: the final error value $\varepsilon$

## 3.5  Attentional Cascade

In spite of the optimal image normalization and feature calculation approaches, to obtain good results in a real-world object detection problem, the *strong classifier* learnt by AdaBoost must be a combination of a large number of *weak classifiers*. Since we need to apply this classifier to a huge number of regions (due to the brute force approach explained in Sect. 3.1.1), the final detection time for an image is prohibitive. In order to address this limitation, Viola and Jones introduced a cascade architecture of multiple *strong classifiers*. The underlying idea is to use only the necessary computation cost in order to reject a non-object image, while more complex analyses are performed in more difficult ones (see Fig. 3.13). The regions that reach the last stage of the cascade and are classified as objects, are selected as object regions, and the rest of the regions are rejected.

Each stage analyzes only the objects accepted by the previous stages, and thus, the non-objects are analyzed only until they are rejected by a detector. The number of applied classifiers is reduced exponentially due to the cascade architecture. Notice that with a false alarm of 0.5, half of the input regions to a stage are rejected, while the other half pass to the next stage. In addition, the stages are *strong classifiers* with weak performance restrictions, and therefore, the number of *weak classifiers* that conform them is smaller.

Learning an *attentional cascade* is not significantly more complex than learning a single *strong classifier*, in the sense that the same algorithm is used, but the training set is changed. Adaboost is used to learn each stage of the cascade, and the rejected samples are replaced by other non-objects which the previous training stages classify by correct objects. The training algorithm for the cascade is shown in Algorithm 7. The final false alarm of the detectors cascade will be $F_{target} = f^n$, where $f$ is the false alarm ratio fixed for each stage of the cascade and $n$ is the number of stages. Analogously, the final hit ratio can be estimated as $d^n$.

---

**Algorithm 7** Attentional Cascade Training Algorithm

---

**Require**: User selected values for $f$, the maximum acceptable false positive rate per layer, the minimum acceptable detection rate per layer $d$, and the target overall false positive rate $F_{target}$. In addition, the algorithm needs a set of positive examples $P$ and a set of negative examples $N$.
Initialize $F_0 = 1.0$ and $D_0 = 1.0$
Set $i = 1$
**while** $F_i > F_{target}$ **do**
  $i \leftarrow i + 1$
  $n_i = 0; F_i = F_{i-1}$
  **while** $F_i > f \times F_{i-1}$ **do**
    $n_i \leftarrow n_i + 1$
    Use $P$ and $N$ to train a classifier with $n_i$ features using Adaboost
    Evaluate current cascaded classifier on validation set to determine $F_i$ and $D_i$
    Decrease threshold for the $i$th classifier until the current cascaded classifier
    has a detection rate of at least $d \times D_{i-1}$ (this also affects $F_i$)
  **endwhile**
  $N \leftarrow 0$
  **if** $F_i > F_{target}$ **then**
    evaluate the current cascaded detector on the set of non-object images and put
    any false detections into the set $N$.
  **endif**
**endwhile**
**Ensure**: A cascade of *strong classifiers*.

---

Certain aspects of the Algorithm 7 should be highlighted. The first one is that the number of negative samples in $N$ needs to be enormous. At each iteration we need to replace the rejected samples with new samples that are mis-classified by previous stages, and as our classifier increases the rejection rate with the number of stages, each time it is more difficult to find new samples. The number of negative examples can be estimated as:

$$N^+ = K + \sum_{i=1}^{S-1} \frac{K \times (1 - f)}{f^i} \tag{3.18}$$

where $S$ is the number of stages, $K$ the number of negative samples we use to train a stage and $f$ the maximum false rate per stage. That is, if we decide to learn a cascade of 10 stages with $f = 0.5$ and $K = 1,000$, which are common values, we need a negative sample set of about 1,024,000 samples. To avoid creating training sets of this dimension, the negative samples are usually collected on-line from image databases or by analyzing TV programs or other large image sources. Summarizing, to learn a cascade of detectors, usually we need to perform the detection process on multiple images.

# References

1. Ullman, S., Sali, E.: Object classification using a fragment-based representation. In: BMVC '00: Proceedings of the First IEEE International Workshop on Biologically Motivated Computer Vision, pp. 73–87. Springer, London (2000)
2. Lowe, D.G.: Object recognition from local scale-invariant features. In: Proceedings of the International Conference on Computer Vision ICCV, pp. 1150–1157. Corfu.citeseer.ist.psu. edu/lowe99object.html (1999)
3. Freund, Y., Schapire, R.E.: Experiments with a new boosting algorithm. In: International Conference on Machine Learning, pp. 148–156 (1996)
4. Ullman, S.: High-level vision. object recognition and visual cognition. A Bradford Book, The MIT Press, New York (1996)
5. Abu-Mostafa, Y.S., Pslatis, D.: Optical neural computing. In: Prieditis, A., Russel, S., (eds.), Scientific American, vol. 256, pp. 66–73 (1987)
6. Binford, T.O.: Inferring surfaces from images. Artif. Intell. **17**, 205–244 (1981)
7. Besl, P.J., Jain, R.C.: Tree-dimentional object recognition. Comput. Surv. **17**, 75–145 (1985)
8. Duin, R.P.W., Roli, F., de Ridder, D.: A note on core research issues for statistical pattern recognition. Pattern Recogn. Lett. **23**(4), 493–499 (2002)
9. Levine, M.D.: Feature extraction: a survey. Proc. IEEE **57**(8), 1391–1407 (1969)
10. Marr, D.: Vision. W.H Freeman, (1982)
11. Marr, D., Hildreth, E.: Theory of edge detection. Proc. R. Soc. Lond. B Biol. Sci. **207**, 187–217 (1980)
12. Canny, J.: A computational approach to edge detection. IEEE Trans. Pattern Anal. Mach. Intell. **8**(6), 679–698 (1986)
13. Deriche, R.: Using canny's criteria to derive a recursively implemented optimal edge detector. Int. J. Comput. Vis. **1**(6), 167–187 (1987)
14. Fleck, M.M.: Multiple widths yield reliable finite differences (computer vision). IEEE Trans. Pattern Anal. Mach. Intell. **14**(4), 412–429 (1992)
15. Viola P., Jones, M.: Rapid object detection using a boosted cascade of simple features. Proc. 2001 IEEE Comput. Soc. Conf. Comput. Vis. Pattern Recogn **1**, 511–518 (2001)
16. Croiser, A., Esteban, D., Galand, C.: Perfect channel splitting by use of interpolation/decimation/tree decomposition techniques. In: Proceedings of the International Symposium Information on Circuits and Systems (1976)
17. Crochiere, R., Weber, S., Flanagan, J.: Digital coding of speech in sub-bands. Bell Syst. Tech. J. **55**, 1069–1085 (1976)

18. Vetterli, M., LeGall, D.: Perfect reconstruction FIR filter banks: some properties and factorizations. IEEE Trans. Acoust. Speech Signal Process. **37**(7), 1057–1071 (1989)
19. Lienhart, R., Maydt, J.: An extended set of haar-like features for rapid object detection. In: Proceedings of the International Conference on Image Processing, pp. 900–903. Rochester, USA, September2002. IEEE. (2002)
20. Balas, B.J., Sinha, P.: Dissociated dipoles: Image representation via non-local comparisons. In: Annual Meeting of the Vision Sciences Society, Sarasota, FL (2003)
21. Balas, B.J., Sinha, P.: Receptive field structures for recognition. Neural Comput. **18**(3), 497–520 (2006)
22. van der Walt, C., Barnard, E.: Data characteristics that determine classifier performance. In: 17th Annual Symposium of the Pattern Recognition Association of South Africa, December (2006)
23. Mitchell, T.M.: Machine Learning. McGraw-Hill, New York (1997)
24. Minsky, M., Papert, S.: Perceptrons pp. 157–169 (1988)
25. Ng, A., Jordan, M.: On discriminative vs. generative classifiers: a comparison of logistic regression and naive bayes. Adv. Neural Inf. Process. Syst. **14**, 841–848 (2002)
26. Jaakkola, T.S., Haussler, D.: Exploiting generative models in discriminative classifiers. In: Proceedings of the 1998 Conference on Advances in Neural Information Processing Systems II, pp. 487–493. MIT Press, Cambridge (1999)
27. Hillel, A.B., Weinshall, D., Hertz, T.: Efficient learning of relational object class models. In: Tenth IEEE International Conference on Computer Vision 2005. ICCV 2005, vol. 2, pp. 1762–1769, Oct 2005
28. Fritz, M., Leibe, B., Caputo, B., Schiele, B.: Integrating representative and discriminant models for object category detection. In: Tenth IEEE International Conference on Computer Vision 2005. ICCV 2005, vol. 2, pp. 1363–1370, Oct 2005
29. Perronnin, F., Dance, C.: Fisher kernels on visual vocabularies for image categorization. In: IEEE Conference on Computer Vision and Pattern Recognition, 2007. CVPR '07, pp. 1–8, June 2007
30. Bosch, A., Zisserman, A., Muñoz, X.: Scene classification using a hybrid generative/discriminative approach. IEEE Trans. Pattern Anal. Mach. Intell. **30**(4), 712–727 (2008)
31. Kearns, M.J., Vazirani, U.V.: An Introduction to Computational Learning Theory. MIT Press, Cambridge (1994)
32. Dietterich, T.G.: (2002) Ensemble learning. In: Ed. Arbib, M.A. (ed.) The Handbook of Brain Theory and Neural Networks. The MIT Press, Cambridge
33. Freund, Y., Schapire, R.E.: A decision-theoretic generalization of on-line learning and an application to boosting. J. Comput. Syst. Sci. **55**(1), 119–139 (1997)
34. Schapire, R.E.: The strength of weak learnability. Mach. Learn. **5**(2), 197–227 (1990)
35. Freund, Y.: Boosting a weak learning algorithm by majority. Inf. Comput. **121**(2), 256–285 (1995)
36. Friedman, J., Hastie, T., Tibshirani, R.: Additive logistic regression: a statistical view of boosting. Ann. Stat. **28**(2), 337–407 (2000)
37. Friedman, J., Stuetzle, W.: Projection pursuit regression. J. Am. Stat. Assoc. **76**(report) 817–823 (1981)
38. Buja, A., Haste, T., Tibshirani, R.: Linear smoothersand additive models. Ann. Stat. **17**, 453–555 (1989)
39. Mita, T., Kaneko, T., Stenger, B., Hori, O.: Discriminative feature co-occurrence selection for object detection. IEEE Trans. Pattern Anal. Mach. Intell. **30**(7), 1257–1269 (2008)
40. Freeman, W.T., Adelson, E.H.: The design and use of steerable filters. IEEE Trans. Pattern Anal. Mach. Intell. **13**(9), 891–906 (1991)
41. Blackmore, S.: The Meme Machine (Popular Science). Oxford University Press, USA (2000)
42. Calvin, W.H.: The six essentials? minimal requirements for the darwinian bootstrapping of quality (1997)

43. Calvin, W.H.: Visual features of intermediate complexity and their use in classification. Nature **330**, 33–34 (1987)
44. Barricelli, N.A.: Esempi numerici di processi di evoluzione. Methodos, 45–68 (1954)
45. Fogel, D.B.: Nils barricelli—artificial life, coevolution, self-adaptation. IEEE Comput. Intell. Mag. **1**(1), 41–45 (2006)
46. Fraser, A.S.: Simulation of genetic systems by automatic digital computers. I. Introduction. Aust. J. Biol. Sci. **10**, 484–491 (1957)
47. Fraser, A.S., Hansche, P.E.: Simulation of genetic systems. major and minor loci. In: Proceedings of the 11th International Congress on Genetics, vol. 3, pp 507–516. Oxford (1965)
48. Fraser, A.S., Burnell, D.: Computer Models in Genetics. McGraw-Hill, New York (1970)
49. Crosby, J.L.: Computer Simulation in Genetics. Wiley, New York (1973)
50. Rechenberg I., (1971) Evolutionsstrategie: optimierung technischer systeme nach prinzipien der biologischen evolution. Ph.D thesis, Technical University of Berlin, Department of Process Engineering
51. Schwefel, H.P.: Numerical Optimization of Computer Models. Wiley, New York (1981)
52. Sedai, S., Rhee, P.K.: Bio-inspired adaboost method for efficient face recognition. In: Frontiers in the Convergence of Bioscience and Information Technologies 2007. FBIT 2007, pp. 715–718, Oct 2007
53. Treptow, A., Zell, A.: Combining adaboost learning and evolutionary search to select features for real-time object detection. In: Congress on Evolutionary Computation 2004. CEC2004, vol. 2, pp. 2107–2113 (2004)
54. Thoresz, K., Sinha, P.: Qualitative representations for recognition. J. Vis. **1**(3), 298–298 (2001)

# Chapter 4
# Traffic Sign Categorization

**Abstract** Since the initials of Artificial Intelligence, many learning techniques have been proposed to deal with many artificial systems. The initial learning designs were proposed to deal with just two classes. Which option is the best one given two previous possibilities? To solve this problem using several examples from two hypotheses, many learning techniques have been developed with successful results. However, in many real applications, it is common to face with problems where $N > 2$ possible solutions exist. Multi-class classification is the term applied to those machine learning problems that require assigning labels to instances where the labels are drawn from a set of at least three classes. Once we have detected a traffic sign, we are in this kind of multi-class scenarios, where we have to discriminate among a set of sign categories. In this chapter, we review state-of-the-art multi-class methodologies based on the Error-Correcting Output Codes framework (ECOC). In particular, we describe different ECOC strategies for extending any kind of classifier to deal the problem of multiclass traffic sign classification.

**Keywords** Traffic sign classification · Multi-class object recognition · Error-correcting output codes · ECOC Coding · ECOC Decoding · Voting · Sub-classes

Nowadays, learning is used to help intelligent systems to interact with their environment and to automatically solve problems without the need of human supervision/interaction. Since the initials of Artificial Intelligence, many learning techniques have been proposed to deal with many artificial systems. The initial learning designs were proposed to deal with just two classes. Which option is the best one given two previous possibilities? To solve this problem using several examples from two hypotheses, many learning techniques have been developed with successful results, such as the ones presented in previous section.

However, in many real applications, it is common to face with problems where $N$ possible solutions (where $N > 3$) exist. Multi-class classification is the term applied to those machine learning problems that require assigning labels to instances where

S. Escalera et al., *Traffic-Sign Recognition Systems*, SpringerBriefs in Computer Science,     53
DOI: 10.1007/978-1-4471-2245-6_4, © Sergio Escalera 2011

the labels are drawn from a set of at least three classes. Once we have detected a traffic sign, we are in this kind of multi-class scenarios, where we have to discriminate among a set of sign categories. If we can design a multi-classifier $h$, then the prediction can be understood as in the binary classification problem, being $h : \boldsymbol{rho} \rightarrow \ell$, where now $\ell = \{\ell_1, .., \ell_N\}$, for a $N$-class problem. Several multi-class classification strategies have been proposed in the literature. However, though there are very powerful binary classifiers, many strategies fail to manage multi-class information. A possible multi-class solution consists of designing and combining of a set of binary classification problems.

## 4.1  Review of Binary Classifiers

In the statistical pattern recognition field considered in this work, classifiers are frequently grouped into those based on similarities, probabilities, or geometric information about class distribution [1].

*Similarity Maximization Methods.* The similarity maximization methods use the similarity between patterns to decide a classification. The main issue in this type of classifiers is the definition of the similarity measure.

*Probabilistic Methods.* The most well known probabilistic methods make use of Bayesian decision theory. The decision rule assigns class labels to that having the maximum posterior probability. The posterior can be calculated by the well-known Bayes rule:

$$\text{posterior} = \frac{\text{likelihood} \times \text{prior}}{\text{evidence}} \tag{4.1}$$

If $P(c_i)$ is the prior probability that a given instance $\rho$ belongs to class $c_i$, $p(\rho|c_i)$ is the class-conditional probability density function: the density for $\rho$ given that the instance is of class $c_i$, and $p(\rho)$ is defined as $\sum p(\rho|c_j) \times P(c_j)$ over all classes. Then, Eq. 4.1 is equivalent to:

$$P(c_j|\rho) = \frac{\mathbf{p}(\rho|\mathbf{c_j}) \times P(\mathbf{c_j})}{\mathbf{p}(\rho)} \tag{4.2}$$

The classification is done in favor of the $j^{\text{th}}$ class is $P(c_j|\rho) > P(\mathbf{c_i}|\rho)$, $\forall c_i \in C$ and $c_i \neq c_j$, where $C$ is the set of classes ($c_j \in C$).

*Geometric Classifiers* Geometric classifiers build decision boundaries by directly minimizing the error criterion.

Table 4.1 summarizes the main classification strategies studied in literature. For each strategy, we show its properties, comments, and type based on the previous grouping.

**Table 4.1** Classification methods

| Method | Property | Comments | Type |
|---|---|---|---|
| Template matching | Assigns patterns to the most similar template | The templates and the metric have to be supplied by the user; the procedure may include nonlinear normalizations; scale (metric) dependent | Similarity maximization |
| Nearest mean classifier | Assigns patterns to the nearest class mean | No training needed; fast testing; scale (metric) dependent | Similarity maximization |
| Subspace method | Assigns patterns to the nearest class subspace | Instead of normalizing on invariants, the subspace of the invariant is used; scale (metric) dependent | Similarity maximization |
| 1-Nearest neighbor rule | Assigns patterns to the class of the nearest training pattern | No training needed; robust performance; slow testing; scale (metric) dependent | Similarity maximization |
| k-Nearest neighbor rule | Assigns Patterns to the majority class among k nearest neighbor using a performance optimized value for k | Asymptotically optimal; scale (metric) dependent, slow testing | Similarity maximization |
| Bayes plug-in | Assigns pattern to the class which has the maximum estimated posterior probability | Yields simple classifiers (linear or quadratic) for Gaussian distributions; sensitive to density estimation errors | Probabilistic |
| Logistic classifier | Maximum likelihood rule for logistic (sigmoidal) posterior probabilities | Linear classifier; iterative procedure; optimal for a family of different distributions (Gaussian); suitable for mixed data types | Probabilistic |
| Parzen classifier | Bayes plug-in rule for Parzen density estimates with performance optimized kernel | Asymptotically optimal; scale (metric) dependent; slow testing | Probabilistic |
| Fisher linear discriminant | Linear classifier using MSE optimization | Simple and fast; similar to Bayes plug-in for Gaussian distributions with identical covariance matrices | Geometric |
| Binary decision tree | Finds a set of thresholds for a pattern-dependent sequence of features | Iterative training procedure; overtraining sensitive; needs pruning; fast testing | Geometric |
| Adaboost | Logistic regression for a combination of weak classifiers | Iterative training procedure; overtraining sensitive; fast training; good generalization performance | Geometric |

(Continued)

**Table 4.1** Continued

| Method | Property | Comments | Type |
|---|---|---|---|
| Perceptron | Iterative optimization of a linear classifier | Sensitive to training parameters; may produce confidence values | Geometric |
| Multi-layer perceptron (Feed-forward neural network) | Iterative MSE optimization of two or more layers of perceptrons (neurons) using sigmoid transfer functions | Sensitive to training parameters; slow training; nonlinear classification function; may produce confidence values; overtraining sensitive; needs regularization | Geometric |
| Radial basis network | Iterative MSE optimization of a feed-forward neural network with at least one layer of neurons using Gaussian-like transfer functions | Sensitive to training parameters; nonlinear classification function; may produce confidence values; overtraining sensitive; needs regularization; may be robust to outliers | Geometric |
| Support vector classifier | Maximizes the margin between the classes by selecting a minimum number of support vectors | Scale (metric) dependent; iterative; slow training; nonlinear; overtraining insensitive; good generalization performance | Geometric |

## 4.2 Multi-Class Classifiers

There are plenty of classification techniques reported in literature for the multi-class problem: Support Vector Machines, decision trees, nearest neighbors rules, etc. Most of the state-of-the-art classification strategies (see Table 4.1) are defined to deal with 2-class problems. Strategies that obtain good generalization performance in the 2-class case, such as Adaboost or Support Vector Machines, have been extended to the multi-class case, but this extension is not always trivial. In such cases, the usual way to proceed is to reduce the complexity of the problem into a set of simpler binary classifiers and combine them. An usual way to combine these simple classifiers is the voting scheme.

Voting (or averaging) is a technique that, instead of using the best hypothesis learnt so far, uses a weighted average of all hypotheses learnt during a training procedure. The averaging procedure is expected to produce more s models, which leads to less overfitting. Some multi-class combining techniques use different classification strategies to split sub-sets of classes and model the classification problem as a combination of different types of decision boundaries in a voting scheme. In this work for multi-class traffic sign categorization, we focus on the combination of classifiers where the base classifier for each individual classification problem of the ensemble is based on the same type of decision boundary. Next, we briefly review the standard voting schemes used in the literature.

### *4.2.1 One Versus the Rest Committee*

To get a $N$-class classifier, it is common to construct a set of binary classifiers $\{h_1, .., h_N\}$, each one trained to split one class from the rest of classes, and use the outputs of each binary classifier to predict one of the $N$ classes [2].

### *4.2.2 One Versus One Committee*

In pairwise classification, we train a classifier for each possible pair of classes [3]. For $N$ classes, this results in $N(N-1)/2$ binary classifiers. This number is usually larger than the number of one-versus-the-rest classifiers; for instance, if $N = 10$, one needs to train 45 binary classifiers rather than 10 as in the one-versus-the-rest strategy. Although this suggests larger training times, the individual problems that we need to train on are significantly smaller, and if the training algorithm scales superlinearly with the training set size, it is actually possible to save time.

Similar considerations apply to the runtime execution speed. When one try to classify a test pattern, we evaluate all 45 binary classifiers, and classify according to which of the classes gets the highest number of votes. A vote for a given class is defined as the classifier putting the pattern into that class. The individual classifiers, however, are usually smaller in size than they would be in the one-versus-the-rest approach. This is for two reasons: first, the training sets are smaller, and second, the problems to be learnt are usually easier, since the classes have less overlap.

### 4.2.3 Error-Correcting Output Codes

Finally, Error-Correcting Output Codes (ECOC) were born as a general framework to combine binary problems to address the multi-class problem. The strategy was introduced by Dietterich and Bakiri [4] in 1995. Based on the error correcting principles [4], ECOC has been successfully applied to a wide range of applications, such as face recognition [5], face verification [6], text recognition [7] or manuscript digit classification [8]. Because of its empirical and theoretical advantages, in this work, we review classical and recent ECOC designs which can be successfully applied in the multi-class traffic sign categorization problem.

Given a set of $N$ classes to be learnt in an ECOC framework, $n$ different bi-partitions (groups of classes) are formed, and $n$ binary problems (dichotomizers) over the partitions are trained. As a result, a codeword of length $n$ is obtained for each class, where each position (bit) of the code corresponds to a response of a given dichotomizer (coded by $+1$ or $-1$ according to their class set membership). Arranging the codewords as rows of a matrix, we define a *coding matrix M*, where $M \in \{-1, +1\}^{N \times n}$ in the binary case. In Fig. 4.1a we show an example of a binary coding matrix $M$. The matrix is coded using 5 dichotomizers $\{h_1, \ldots, h_5\}$ for a 4-class problem $\{c_1, \ldots, c_4\}$ of respective codewords $\{y_1, \ldots, y_4\}$. The hypotheses are trained by considering the labeled training data samples $\{(\rho_1, l(\rho_1)), \ldots, (\rho_m, l(\rho_m))\}$ for a set of $m$ data samples. The white regions of the coding matrix $M$ are coded by $+1$ (considered as one class for its respective dichotomizer $h_j$), and the dark regions are coded by $-1$ (considered as the other one). For example, the first classifier is trained to discriminate $c_3$ against $c_1$, $c_2$, and $c_4$; the second one classifies $c_2$ and $c_3$ against $c_1$ and $c_4$, etc., as follows:

$$h_1(\rho) = \begin{cases} 1 & \text{if } \rho \in \{c_3\} \\ -1 & \text{if } \rho \in \{c_1, c_2, c_4\} \end{cases}, \ldots, \quad h_5(\rho) = \begin{cases} 1 & \text{if } \rho \in \{c_2, c_4\} \\ -1 & \text{if } \rho \in \{c_1, c_3\} \end{cases} \quad (4.3)$$

During the decoding process, applying the $n$ binary classifiers, a code $x$ is obtained for each data sample $\rho$ in the test set. This code is compared to the base codewords $(y_i, i \in [1, .., N])$ of each class defined in the matrix $M$. And the data sample is assigned to the class with the *closest* codeword. In Fig. 4.1(a), the new code $x$ is compared to the class codewords $\{y_1, \ldots, y_4\}$ using the Hamming [2] and the Euclidean Decoding [9]. The test sample is classified by class $c_2$ in both cases, correcting one bit error.

In the ternary symbol-based ECOC, the coding matrix becomes $M_{i,j} \in \{-1, 0, +1\}$. In this case, the symbol zero means that a particular class is not considered for a given classifier. A ternary coding design is shown in Fig. 4.1b. The matrix is coded using 7 dichotomizers $\{h_1, \ldots, h_7\}$ for a 4-class problem $\{c_1, \ldots, c_4\}$ of respective codewords $\{y_1, \ldots, y_4\}$. The white regions are coded by 1 (considered as one class by the

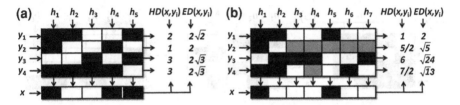

**Fig. 4.1 a** Binary ECOC design for a 4-class problem. An input test codeword $x$ is classified by class $c_2$ using the Hamming or the Euclidean Decoding. **b** Example of a ternary matrix $M$ for a 4-class problem. A new test codeword $x$ is classified by class $c_1$ using the Hamming and the Euclidean Decoding

respective dichotomizer $h_j$), the dark regions by $-1$ (considered as the other class), and the grey regions correspond to the zero symbol (classes that are not considered by the respective dichotomizer $h_j$). For example, the first classifier is trained to discriminate $c_3$ against $c_1$ and $c_2$ without taking into account class $c_4$, the second one classifies $c_2$ against $c_1$, $c_3$, and $c_4$, etc. In this case, the Hamming and Euclidean Decoding classify the test data sample by class $c_1$. Note that a test codeword can not contain the zero value since the output of each dichotomizer is $h_j \in \{-1, +1\}$.

The analysis of the ECOC error evolution has demonstrated that ECOC corrects errors caused by the bias and the variance of the learning algorithm [10].[1] The variance reduction is to be expected, since ensemble techniques address this problem successfully and ECOC is a form of voting procedure. On the other hand, the bias reduction must be interpreted as a property of the decoding step. It follows that if a point $\rho$ is misclassified by some of the learnt dichotomies, it can still be classified correctly after being decoded due to the correction ability of the ECOC algorithm. Non-local interaction between training examples leads to different bias errors. Initially, the experiments in [10] show the bias and variance error reduction for algorithms with *global* behavior (when the errors made at the output bits are not correlated). After that, new analysis also shows that ECOC can improve performance of *local* classifiers (e.g., the $k$-nearest neighbor, which yields correlated predictions across the output bits) by extending the original algorithm or selecting different features for each bit [11].

## 4.3 Error-Correcting Output Codes: Coding Designs

In this section, we review the state-of-the-art on coding designs. We divide the designs based on their membership to the binary or the ternary ECOC frameworks.

---

[1] The bias term describes the component of the error that results from systematic errors of the learning algorithm. The variance term describes the component of the error that results from random variation and noise in the training samples and random behavior of the learning algorithm. For more details, see [10].

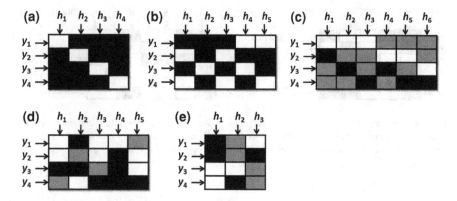

**Fig. 4.2** Coding designs for a 4-class problem: **a** one-versus-all, **b** dense random, **c** one-versus-one, **d** sparse random, and **e** DECOC

### 4.3.1 Binary Coding

The standard binary coding designs are the one-versus-all [2] strategy and the dense random strategy [9]. In one-versus-all, each dichotomizer is trained to distinguish one class from the rest of classes. Given $N$ classes, this technique has a codeword length of $N$ bits. An example of an one-versus-all ECOC design for a 4-class problem is shown in Fig. 4.2a. The dense random strategy generates a high number of random coding matrices $M$ of length $n$, where the values $\{+1, -1\}$ have a certain probability to appear (usually $P(1) = P(-1) = 0.5$). Studies on the performance of the dense random strategy suggested a length of $n = 10 \log N$ [9]. For the set of generated dense random matrices, the optimal one should maximize the Hamming Decoding measure between rows and columns (also considering the opposites), taking into account that each column of the matrix $M$ must contain the two different symbols $\{-1, +1\}$. An example of a dense random ECOC design for a 4-class problem and five dichotomizers is shown in Fig. 4.2b. The complete coding approach was also proposed in [9]. Nevertheless, it requires the complete set of classifiers to be measured $(2^{N-1} - 1)$, which usually is computationally unfeasible in practice.

### 4.3.2 Ternary Coding

The standard ternary coding designs are the one-versus-one strategy [3] and the sparse random strategy [9]. The one-versus-one strategy considers all possible pairs of classes, thus, its codeword length is of $\frac{N(N-1)}{2}$. An example of an one-versus-one ECOC design for a 4-class problem is shown in Fig. 4.2c. The sparse random strategy is similar to the dense random design, but it includes the third symbol zero with another probability to appear, given by $P(0) = 1 - P(-1) - P(1)$. Studies suggested a sparse code length of $15 \log N$ [9]. An example of a sparse ECOC design

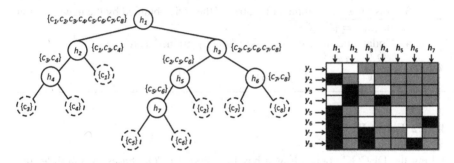

**Fig. 4.3** Example of a binary tree structure and its DECOC codification

for a 4-class problem and five dichotomizers is shown in Fig. 4.2d. In the ternary case, the complete coding approach can also be defined.

Due to the huge number of bits involved in the traditional coding strategies, new problem-dependent designs have been proposed [12–14]. The new techniques are based on exploiting the problem domain by selecting the representative binary problems that increase the generalization performance while keeping the code length small.

### 4.3.2.1 Discriminant ECOC (DECOC)

Is based on the embedding of discriminant tree structures derived from the problem domain. The binary trees are built by looking for the sub-sets of classes that maximizes the mutual information between the data and their respective class labels. As a result, the length of the codeword is only $(n - 1)$. The algorithm is summarized in Algorithm 8. In Fig. 4.3, a binary tree structure for an 8-class problem is shown. Each node of the tree splits a sub-set of classes. Each internal node is embedded in the ECOC matrix as a column, where the white regions correspond to the classes on the left sub-sets of the tree, the black regions to the classes on the right sub-sets of the tree, and the grey regions correspond to the non-considered classes (set to zero). Another example of a DECOC design for a 4-class problem obtained by embedding a balanced tree is shown in Fig. 4.2e.

---

**Algorithm 8** DECOC algorithm.

---

**DECOC:** Create the Column Code Binary Tree as follows:
Initialize $L$ to $L_0 = \{\{c_1, .., c_N\}\}$
**while** $|L_k| > 0$

1) Get $S_k : S_k \in L_k, k \in [0, N - 2]$
2) Find the optimal binary partition $BP(S_k)$ that maximizes the fast quadratic mutual information [14].

3) Assign to the column $t$ of matrix $M$ the code obtained by the new partition $BP(S_k) = \{C_1, C_2\}$.

4) Update the sub-sets of classes $L_k$ to be trained as follows:
$$L'_k = L_k \backslash S_k$$
$$L_{k+1} = L'_k \cup C_i \text{ iff } |C_i| > 1, i \in [1, 2]$$

### 4.3.2.2 Forest-ECOC

Taking the DECOC approach as a baseline, Forest-ECOC bases on multiple tree embedding. The method builds an optimal tree–the one with the highest classification score at each node–and several suboptimal trees– the ones closer to the optimal one under certain conditions. Let us keep at each iteration the best $k$ partitions of the set of classes. If the best partition is used to construct the current ECOC tree, the rest of partitions form the roots of $k - 1$ trees. We repeat iteratively this process until all nodes from the trees are decomposed into one class. Given a base classifier, the sub-optimal tree candidates are designed to have the maximum classification score at each node without repeating previous sub-partitions of classes. In the case of generating $T$ first optimal trees, we can create an ensemble of trees by embedding them in the ECOC matrix, as shown in Algorithm 9.

---

**Algorithm 9** Training algorithm for the Forest-ECOC.

---

Given $N$ classes: $c_1, \ldots, c_N$ and $T$ trees to be embedded
for $t = 1, .., T$ do
    Initialize the tree root with the set $N_0 = \{c_1, \ldots, c_N\}$
    $i \Leftarrow 0$
    Generate the best tree at iteration $t$:
    for each node $N_i$ do
        Train the best partition of its set of classes $\{C_1, C_2\}|N_i = C_1 \cup C_2$ using a classifier $h_i$ (if the sub-partition has not been previously considered) so that the training error is minimal
    end for
    According to the partition obtained at each node, codify each column of the matrix $M$ as:
$$M(r, i) = \begin{cases} 0 & \text{if } c_r \notin N_i \\ +1 & \text{if } c_r \in C_1 \\ -1 & \text{if } c_r \in C_2 \end{cases}$$

    where $r$ is the index of the corresponding class $c_r$
    $i \Leftarrow i + 1$ end for

---

This technique provides a sub-optimal solution because of the combination of robust classifiers obtained from a greedy search using the classification score. One of the main advantages of this technique is that the trees share their information among classes in the ECOC matrix $M$. It is done at the decoding step by considering all the coded positions of a class jointly instead of separately. It is easy to see that each tree structure of $N$ classes introduces $N - 1$ classifiers, that is far from the $\frac{N(N-1)}{2}$ dichotomizers required for the one-versus-one coding strategy.

An example of two optimal-trees and the Forest-ECOC matrix for a toy problem is shown in Fig. 4.4. The Fig 4.4a and b show two examples of optimal trees. The second optimal tree is constructed based on the following optimal sub-partitions of classes. In this way, for the first initial set of classes $\{c_1, c_2, c_3, c_4\}$, the two optimal trees include the best sub-partitions of classes in terms of the classification score, that in the example corresponds to $c_1, c_3$ vs $c_2, c_4$ for the first tree, and $c_1, c_2, c_3$ vs $c_4$ for the second tree, respectively. Figure 4.4c shows the embedding of trees into the Forest-ECOC matrix $M$. Note that the column $h_3$ corresponds to the node $N_3$, and the following dichotomizers correspond to the nodes of the second tree. The classes that do not belong to the sub-partitions of classes are set to zero. On the other hand, the classes belonging to each partition are set to $+1$ and $-1$ values, defining the subset of classes involved on each classifier.

Given an input sample to test with the Forest-ECOC matrix, we obtain the Forest-ECOC vector where each vector component is the result of solving each binary classifier trained on each of the columns of the matrix.

The second step of the ECOC process is the decoding. Here we can apply any decoding strategy (from the ternary framework explained later) to decode a Forest-ECOC design.

### 4.3.2.3  ECOC Optimum Node Embedding

The ECOC-ONE technique is motivated by the necessity of having fast algorithms with high discriminative power able to generate as much as necessary number of dichotomizers in order to obtain the desired performance. The work of [14] has motivated the look for techniques with small codeword length that provide high performance in general conditions. The ECOC-ONE is a general procedure to increase the accuracy of any ECOC coding by adding very few optimal dichotomizers. In this sense, if the original coding has small length, the extension after the ECOC-ONE results in a still compact codewords but with increased performance. In particular, we describe the ECOC-ONE extension to optimize the initial embedded tree of a DECOC design.

*ECOC-ONE definition.* ECOC-Optimal Node Embedding defines a general procedure capable of extending any coding matrix by adding dichotomizers based on a discriminability criterion. In the case of a multiclass recognition problem, this procedure starts with a given ECOC coding matrix. We increase this ECOC matrix in an iterative way, adding dichotomizers that correspond to different sub-partitions of classes. These partitions are found using greedy optimization based on the confusion

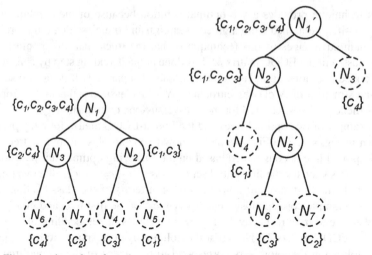

First optimal tree for a four-class problem  Second optimal tree for the same problem

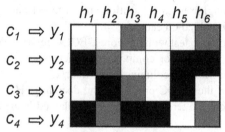

Forest-ECOC matrix $M$ for the problem, where $h_1$, $h_2$ and $h_3$ correspond
to classifiers of $N_1$, $N_2$ and $N_3$ from the first tree, and $h_4$, $h_5$ and $h_6$ to $N'_1$, $N'_2$
and $N'_5$ from the second tree

**Fig. 4.4**  Four-class optimal trees and the Forest-ECOC matrix

matrices so that the ECOC accuracy improves on both training and validation sets.
The training set guides the convergence process, and the validation set is used to avoid
overfitting and to select a configuration of the learning procedure that maximizes the
generalization performance. Since not all problems require the same dichotomizers
structure -in form of sub-partitions-, the optimal node embedding approach generates an optimal ECOC-ONE matrix dependent on the hypothesis performance in a
specific problem domain.

*Optimizing node embedding.* In order to explain the procedure, we divide the
ECOC-ONE algorithm in 6 steps: optimal tree generation, weights estimation, accu-
racy estimate based on confusion matrix, defining the new optimal dichotomizer, and
ECOC matrix $M$ construction.

Let us define the notation used in the following paragraphs: given a data pair
$(\rho, l)$, where $s$ is a multidimensional data point and $l$ is the label associated to that

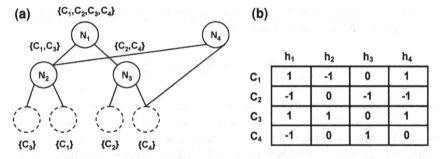

**Fig. 4.5 a** Optimal tree and first optimal node embedded, **b** ECOC-ONE code matrix $M$ for four dichotomizers

sample, we define $S = \{(\rho, l)\} = \{(\rho_t, l_t)\} \bigcup \{(\rho_v, l_v)\}$, where $S_t = \{(\rho_t, l_t)\}$ and $S_v = \{(\rho_v, l_v)\}$ are the sets of data pairs associated to training and validation sets, respectively. In the same way, $\varepsilon(h(\rho), l)$ represents the empirical error over the data set $\rho$ given an hypothesis $h(\cdot)$.

(a) *Optimal tree generation.* We show the use of a binary tree structure using accuracy as a sub-partition splitting criterion. We initialize the root of the tree with the set containing all the classes. Afterwards, for the tree building, each node of the tree is generated by an exhaustive search[2] of the sub-partition of classes associated to the parent node, so that the classifier using that sub-partition of classes attains maximal accuracy on the training and validation subsets. In Fig. 4.5, the sub-partition of classes required at each node of the optimal tree is shown. For example, given the root node containing all classes, the optimal partition achieving the least error is given by $\{\{c_1 \cup c_3\}, \{c_2 \cup c_4\}\}$. Once we have generated the optimal tree, we embed each internal node of the tree into the coding matrix $M$ in the following way: consider the partition of the set of classes associated to a node $C = \{C_1 \cup C_2 | C_1 \cap C_2 = \emptyset\}$. The element $(i, r)$ of the ECOC-ONE matrix corresponding to class $i$ and dichotomizer $r$ is given by:

$$M(i, r) = \begin{cases} 0 & \text{if } c_i \notin C \\ +1 & \text{if } c_i \in C_1 \\ -1 & \text{if } c_i \in C_2 \end{cases} \tag{4.4}$$

Although this strategy is the one chosen to explain the ECOC-ONE design, note that any coding could be used instead.

(b) *Weights estimates.* It is known that when a multiclass classification problem is decomposed into binary problems, not all of these base classifiers have the same importance. In this way, ECOC-ONE introduces a weight to adjust the importance of each dichotomizer in the ensemble ECOC matrix. In particular, the weight associated

---

[2] In the case that the number of classes makes the exhaustive computation unfeasible we can use SFFS as explained in [14].

to each column depends on the error when applying the ECOC to both training sets (training and validation) in the following way,

$$w_i = 0.5 \log \left( \frac{1 - \varepsilon(h_i(\rho), l)}{\varepsilon(h_i(\rho), l)} \right) \tag{4.5}$$

where $w_i$ is the weight for the $i^{\text{th}}$ dichotomizer, and $\varepsilon(h_i(\rho), l)$ is the error produced by this dichotomizer at the affected classes on both sets of the partition. This equation is based on the weighted scheme of the additive logistic regression [15]. In the following section, we explain how we select the dichotomizers and how their weights affect the convergence of the algorithm.

(c) *Test accuracy of the training and validation sets.* Once constructed the binary tree and its corresponding coding matrix, we look for additional dichotomizers in order to focus on the examples that are difficult to classify. To select the next optimal node, we test the current $M$ accuracy on $S_t$ and $S_v$ resulting in $a_t$ and $a_v$, respectively. We combine both accuracies in the following way:

$$a_{\text{total}} = \frac{1}{2}(a_t + a_v)$$

In order to find each accuracy value, we obtain the resulting codeword $x \in \{-1, 1\}^n$ using the strong hypothesis $\mathscr{H} = \{h_1, \ldots, h_j\}$ for each sample of these sets, and we label it as follows:

$$\tilde{I} = \operatorname{argmin}_j \ \left( d(x, y_j) \right) \tag{4.6}$$

where $d(\cdot)$ is a distance estimation between codeword $x$ and the codeword $y_j$. $\mathscr{H}(M, h, \rho)$ is the strong hypothesis resulted from the application of the set of learning algorithms $h(\cdot)$ on the problems defined by each column of the ECOC matrix $M$ on a data point $\rho$. The result of $\mathscr{H}(M, h, \rho)$ is an estimated codeword $x$.

(d) *The training and validation confusion matrices.* Once we test the accuracy of the strong hypothesis $\mathscr{H}$ on $S_t$ and $S_v$, we estimate their respective confusion matrices $v_t(\mathbf{S_t})$ and $v_v(\mathbf{S_v})$. Both confusion matrices are of size $N \times N$, and have at position $(i, j)$ the number of instances of class $c_i$ classified as class $c_j$.

$$v_k(i, j) =| \{(\rho, l)_k : l = c_i, h(\rho) = c_j\} |, k = \{t, v\} \tag{4.7}$$

where $l$ is the label estimation. Once the matrices have been obtained, we select the pair $\{c_i, c_j\}$ with maximal value according to the following expression:

$$\{c_i, c_j\} = \operatorname{argman}_{c_i, c_j; i \neq j} \left( v_t(i, j) + v_t^T(i, j) + v_v(i, j) + v_v^T(i, j) \right) \tag{4.8}$$

$\forall(i, j) \in [1, \ldots, N]$, where $v^T$ is the transposed matrix of $v$. The resulting pair is the set of classes that are most easily confounded, and therefore they have the maximum partial empirical error

(e) *Find the new dichotomizer*. Once the set of classes $\{c_i, c_j\}$ with maximal error has been obtained, we create a new column of the ECOC matrix. Each candidate column considers a possible sub-partition of classes,

$$\wp = \{\{\{c_i\} \bigcup C_1\}, \{\{c_j\} \bigcup C_2\}\} \subseteq C \text{ so that } C_1 \cap C_2 \cap c_i \cap c_j = \oslash \text{ and } C_i \subseteq C.$$

In particular, we are looking for the subset division of classes $\wp$ so that the dichotomizer $h_t$ associated to that division minimizes the empirical error defined by $\varepsilon(\mathscr{H}(\rho), l)$.

$$\widetilde{\wp} = \operatorname{argmin}_{\wp} \left( \varepsilon(\mathscr{H}(\rho), l) \right) \tag{4.9}$$

Once defined the new sets of classes, the column components associated to the set $\{\{c_i\}, C_1\}$ are set to $+1$, the components of the set $\{\{c_j\}, C_2\}$ are set to $-1$ and the positions of the rest of classes are set to zero. In the case that multiple candidates obtain the same performance, the one involving more classes is preferred. Firstly, it reduces the number of uncertainty in the ECOC matrix by reducing the number of zeros in the dichotomizer. Secondly, one can see that when more classes are involved, the generalization achieved is greater. Each dichotomizer finds a more complex rule on a greater number of classes. This fact has also been observed in the work of Torralba et al. [16]. In their work, a multi-task scheme is presented that yields to a classifier with an improved generalization by aids of class grouping algorithms.

(f) *Update the matrix*. The column $m_i$ is added to the matrix $M$ and its weight $w_i$ is calculated using Eq. 4.5.

---

**Algorithm 10** ECOC-ONE general algorithm

---

Given $N_c$ classes and a coding matrix $M$:
**while** *error* $> \varepsilon$ or *error*$_t$ $<$ *error*$_{t-1}$, $t \in [1, T]$:
    Compute the optimal node $t$:

    1) Test accuracy on the training and validation sets $S_t$ and $S_v$.
    2) Select the pair of classes $\{c_i, c_j\}$ with the highest error analyzing the confusion matrices from $S_t$ and $S_v$.
    3) Find the partition $\wp_t = \{C_1, C_2\}$ that minimizes the error rate in $S_t$ and $S_v$.
    4) Compute the weight for the dichotomizer of partition $\wp_i$ based on its classification score.

    Update the matrix $M$.

---

Algorithm 10 shows the summarized steps for the ECOC-ONE approach. Note that, the process described is iterated while the error on the training subsets is greater than $\varepsilon$ or the number of iterations $i \leq T$.

*ECOC-ONE example.* An example of an ECOC-ONE strategy applied to a four-class classification example can be found in Fig. 4.5. The initial optimal tree corresponds to the dichotomizers of optimal sub-partition of the classes. This tree has been generated using accuracy as a sub-partition splitting criterion. After testing the performance of the ensemble tree (composed by the columns $\{h_1, h_2, h_3\}$ of the ECOC matrix $M$ of Fig. 4.5b), let assume that classes $\{c_2, c_3\}$ get maximal error in the confusion matrices $v_t$ and $v_v$. We search for the sub-partition of classes using the training and validation subsets so that the error between $\{c_2, c_3\}$ and all previous misclassified samples is minimized. Suppose now that this sub-partition is $\{c_1, c_3\}$ versus $\{c_2\}$. As a result, a new node $N_4$ corresponding to dichotomizer $h_4$ is created. We can observe in Fig. 4.5 that $N_4$ uses a class partition that is present in the tree. In this sense, this new node connects two different nodes of the tree. Note that using the previously included dichotomizers, the partition $\{c_1, c_3\}$ is solved by $N_2$. In this way, the Hamming distance between $c_2$ and $c_3$ is increased by adding the new dichotomizer to the whole structure. At the same time, the distance among the rest of the classes is usually maintained or slightly modified.

One of the desirable properties of the ECOC matrix is to have maximal distance between rows. In this sense, ECOC-ONE procedure focuses on the relevant difficult partitions, increasing the distance between "close" classes. This fact improves the robustness of the method since difficult classes are likely to have a greater number of dichotomizers centered on them. In this sense, it creates different geometrical arrangements of decision boundaries, and leads the dichotomizers to make different bias errors.

### 4.3.2.4 Sub-Class ECOC

Considering the training data in the process of the ECOC design allows to obtain compact codewords with high classification performance. However, the final accuracy is still based on the ability of the base classifier to learn each individual problem. Difficult problems, those which the base classifier is not able to find a solution for, require the use of high capacity classifiers, such as Support Vector Machines with Radial Basis Function kernel [17], and expensive parameter optimizations. Look at the example of Fig. 4.6a. A linear classifier is used to split two classes. In this case, the base classifier is not able to find a convex solution. On the other hand, in Fig. 4.6b, one of the previous classes has been split into two sub-sets, that we call *sub-classes*. Then, the original problem is solved using two linear classifiers, and the two new sub-classes have the same original class label. Some studies in the literature tried to form sub-classes using the labels information, which is called Supervised Clustering [18,19]. In these types of systems, clusters are usually formed without taking into account the behavior of the base classifier that learns the data. In a recent work [20], the authors use the class labels to form the sub-classes that improve the performance of particular Discriminant Analysis algorithms.

In this section, we review a problem-dependent ECOC design where classes are partitioned into sub-classes using a clustering approach for the cases that the base

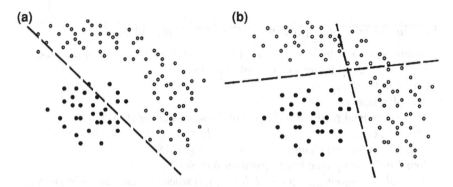

**Fig. 4.6 a** Decision boundary of a linear classifier of a 2-class problem. **b** Decision boundaries of a linear classifier splitting the problem of (a) into two more simple tasks

classifier is not capable to distinguish the classes (eg. similar visual traffic signs). Sequential Forward Floating Search based on maximizing the Mutual Information is used to generate the sub-groups of problems that are split into more simple ones until the base classifier is able to learn the original problem. In this way, multi-class problems which can not be modeled by using the original set of classes are modeled without the need of using more complex classifiers. The final ECOC design is obtained by combining the sub-problems.

From an initial set of classes $C$ of a given multi-class problem, the objective of the sub-class ECOC strategy is to define a new set of classes $C'$, where $|C'| > |C|$, so that the new set of binary problems is easier to learn for a given base classifier. For this purpose, we use a guided procedure that, in a problem-dependent way, groups classes and splits them into sub-sets if necessary.

Look at the 3-class problem shown on the top of Fig. 4.7a. The standard DECOC algorithm [14] considers the whole set of classes to split it into two sub-sets of classes $\wp^+$ and $\wp^-$ maximizing the *MI* criterion on a sequential forward floating search procedure (*SFFS*). In the example, the first sub-sets found correspond to $\wp^+ = \{C_1, C_2\}$ and $\wp^- = \{C_3\}$. Then, a base classifier is used to train its corresponding dichotomizer $h_1$. This classifier is shown in the node $h_1$ of the tree structure shown in Fig. 4.7d. The procedure is repeated until all classes are split into separate sub-sets $\wp$. In the example, the second classifier is trained to split the sub-sets of classes $\wp^+ = C_1$ from $\wp^- = C_2$ because the classes $C_1$ and $C_2$ were still contained in a single sub-set after the first step. This second classifier is codified by the node $h_2$ of Fig. 4.7d. When the tree is constructed, the coding matrix $M$ is obtained by codifying each internal node of the tree as a column of the coding matrix (see Fig. 4.7c).

In our case, sequential forward floating search (*SFFS*) is also applied to look for the sub-sets $\wp^+$ and $\wp^-$ that maximizes the mutual information between the data and their respective class labels [14]. The encoding algorithm is shown in Algorithm 11.

---

**Algorithm 11** Problem-dependent Sub-Class ECOC algorithm.

---

**Inputs**: $J, C, \theta = \{\theta_{size}, \theta_{perf}, \theta_{impr}\}$ Thresholds for the number of samples, performance, and improvement between iterations

**Outputs**: $C', J', \wp', M$

**[Initialization:]**

Create the trivial partition $\{\wp_0^+, \wp_0^-\}$ of the set of classes $\{C_i\}$: $\{\wp_0^+, \wp_0^-\} = \{\{\emptyset\}, \{C_1, C_2, \ldots, C_N\}\}$ $L_0 = \{\wp_0^-\}$ $J' = J$; $C' = C$; $\wp' = \emptyset$; $M = \emptyset$; $k = 1$

**Step 1** $S_k$ is the first element of $L_{k-1}$ $L'_k = L_{k-1} \backslash \{S_k\}$

**Step 2** Find the optimal binary partition $BP(S_k)$:

$\{\wp_k^+, \wp_k^-\} = argmax_{BP(S_k)}(I(\mathbf{x}, d(BP(S_k))))$ where $I$ is the mutual information criterion, $\mathbf{x}$ is the random variable associated to the features and $d$ is the discrete random variable of the dichotomizer labels, defined in the following terms,

$$d = d(\mathbf{x}, BP(S_k)) = \begin{cases} 1 & \text{if } \mathbf{X} \in C_i | C_i \in \wp_k^+ \\ -1 & \text{if } \mathbf{X} \in C_i | C_i \in \wp_k^- \end{cases}$$

**Step 3** // Look for sub-classes

$\{C', J', \wp'\} = SPLIT(J_{p_k^+}, J_{p_k^-}, C', J', J, \wp', \theta)$

**Step 4** $L_k = \{L'_k \cup \wp_k^i\}$ if $|\wp_k^i| > 1$ $\forall i \in \{+, -\}$

**Step 5** If $|L_k| \neq 0$

$k = k + 1$ **go to Step 1**

**Step 6** Codify the coding matrix $M$ using each partition $\{\wp_i^+, \wp_i^-\}$ of $\wp'$, $i \in [1, .., |\wp'|]$ and each class $C_r \in \wp_i = \{\wp_i^+ \cup \wp_i^-\}$ as follows:

$$M(C_r, i) = \begin{cases} 0 & \text{if } C_r \notin \wp_i \\ +1 & \text{if } C_r \in \wp_i^+ \\ -1 & \text{if } C_r \in \wp_i^- \end{cases} \tag{4.10}$$

---

Given a $N$-class problem, the whole set of classes is used to initialize the set $L$ containing the sets of labels for the classes to be learned. At the beginning of each iteration $k$ of the algorithm (**Step 1**), the first element of $L$ is assigned to $S_k$ in the first step of the algorithm. Next, *SFFS* is used to find the optimal binary partition $BP$ of $S_k$ that maximizes the mutual information $I$ between the data and their respective class labels (**Step 2**). The *SFFS* algorithm used can be found in [21].

To illustrate the procedure, let us return to the example of the top of Fig. 4.7a. On the first iteration of the sub-class ECOC algorithm, *SFFS* finds the sub-set $\wp^+ = \{C_1, C_2\}$ against $\wp^- = \{C_3\}$. The encoding of this problem is shown in the first matrix of Fig. 4.7c. The positions of the column corresponding to the classes of the first partition are coded by $+1$ and the classes corresponding to the second partition to $-1$, respectively. In our procedure, the base classifier is used to test if the performance obtained by the trained dichotomizers is sufficient. Observe the decision boundaries of the picture next to the first column of the matrix in Fig. 4.7b. One can see that the base classifier finds a good solution for this first problem.

Then, the second classifier is trained to split $\wp^+ = C_1$ against $\wp^- = C_2$, and its performance is computed. To separate the current sub-sets is not a trivial problem, and the classification performance is poor. Therefore, our procedure tries to split the data $J_{\wp^+}$ and $J_{\wp^-}$ from the current sub-sets $\wp^+$ and $\wp^-$ into more simple sub-sets. At **Step 3** of the algorithm, the splitting criteria $SC$ takes as input a data set $J_{\wp^+}$ or $J_{\wp^-}$ from a sub-set $\wp^+$ or $\wp^-$, and splits it into two sub-sets $J_{\wp^+}^+$ and $J_{\wp^+}^-$ or $J_{\wp^-}^+$ and $J_{\wp^-}^-$. The splitting algorithm is shown in Algorithm 12.

---

**Algorithm 12** Sub-Class *SPLIT* algorithm.

---

**Inputs:** $J_{\wp^1}, J_{\wp^2}, C', J', J, \wp', \theta$ // $C'$ is the final set of classes, $J'$ the data for the final set of classes, and $\wp'$ is the labels for all the partitions of classes of the final set.
**Outputs:** $C', J', \wp'$
**Step 1** Split problems:
$\{J_{\wp^+}^+, J_{\wp^+}^-\} = SC(J_{\wp^+})^3$
$\{J_{\wp^-}^+, J_{\wp^-}^-\} = SC(J_{\wp^-})$
**Step 2** Select sub-classes:
if $|J_{\wp^+}^+, J_{\wp^+}^-| > |J_{\wp^-}^+, J_{\wp^-}^-|$ // find the largest distance between the means of each sub-set.
$\{J_+^+, J_+^-\} = \{J_{\wp^+}^+, J_{\wp^-}\}; \{J_-^+, J_-^-\} = \{J_{\wp^+}^+, J_{\wp^-}\}$
else
$\{J_+^+, J_+^-\} = \{J_{\wp^-}^+, J_{\wp^+}\}; \{J_-^+, J_-^-\} = \{J_{\wp^-}^-, J_{\wp^+}\}$
end
**Step 3** Test parameters to continue splitting:
if $TEST\_PARAMETERS(J_{\wp^1}, J_{\wp^2}, J_1^1, J_1^2, J_2^1, J_2^2, \theta)$ // call the function with the new sub-sets
$\{C', J', \wp'\} = SPLIT(J_1^1, J_1^2, C', J', J, \wp', \theta)$
$\{C', J', \wp'\} = SPLIT(J_2^1, J_2^2, C', J', J, \wp', \theta)$
end
**Step 4** Save the current partition:
Update the data for the new sub-classes and previous sub-classes if intersections exists $J'$.
Update the final number of sub-classes $C'$.
Create $\wp_c = \{\wp_{c^1}, \wp_{c^2}\}$ the set of labels of the current partition.
Update the labels of the previous partitions $\wp$.
Update the set of partitions labels with the new partition $\wp' = \wp' \cup \wp_c$.

---

When two data sub-sets $\{J_{\wp^+}^+, J_{\wp^+}^-\}$ and $\{J_{\wp^-}^+, J_{\wp^-}^-\}$ are obtained, only one of both split sub-sets is used. We select the sub-sets that have the highest distance between the means of each cluster. Suppose that the distance between $J_{\wp^-}^+$ and $J_{\wp^-}^-$ is larger

---

[3] $SC$ corresponds to the splitting method of the input data into two main clusters.

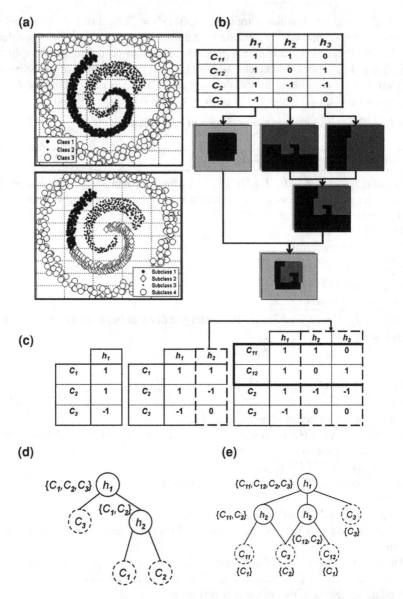

**Fig. 4.7** **a** Top: Original 3-class problem. Bottom: 4 sub-classes found. **b** Sub-Class ECOC encoding using the four sub-classes using Discrete Adaboost with 40 runs of Decision Stumps. **c** Learning evolution of the sub-class matrix $M$. **d** Original tree structure without applying sub-class. **e** New tree-based configuration using sub-classes

than between $J^+_{\wp+}$ and $J^-_{\wp+}$. Then, only $J_{\wp+}$, $J^+_{\wp-}$, and $J^-_{\wp-}$ are used. If the new sub-sets improve the classification performance, new sub-classes are formed, and the process is repeated.

In the example of Fig. 4.7, applying the splitting criteria $SC$ over the two sub-sets, two clusters are found for $\wp^+ = C_1$ and for $\wp^- = C_2$. Then, the original encoding of the problem $C_1$ vs $C_2$ (corresponding to the second column of the matrix in the center of Fig. 4.7c) is split into two columns marked with the dashed lines in the matrix on the right. In this way, the original $C_1$ vs $C_2$ problem is transformed to two more simple problems $\{C_{11}\}$ against $\{C_2\}$ and $\{C_{12}\}$ against $\{C_2\}$. Here the first subindex of the class corresponds to the original class, and the second subindex to the number of sub-class. It implies that the class $C_1$ is split into two sub-classes (look at the bottom of Fig. 4.7a), and the original 3-class problem $C = \{C_1, C_2, C_3\}$ becomes the 4-subclass problem $C' = \{C_{11}, C_{12}, C_2, C_3\}$. As the class $C_1$ has been decomposed by the splitting of the second problem, we need to save the information of the current sub-sets and the previous sub-sets affected by the new splitting. The steps to update this information are summarized in the **Step 4** of the splitting algorithm. We use the object labels to define the set of sub-classes of the current partition $\wp_c$. If new sub-classes are created, the set of sub-classes $C'$ and the data for sub-classes $J'$ have to be updated. Note that when a class or a sub-class previously considered for a given binary problem is split in a future iteration of the procedure, the labels from the previous sub-sets $\{\wp^+, \wp^-\}$ need to be updated with the new information. Finally, the set of labels for the binary problems $\wp'$ is updated with the labels of the current sub-set $\wp' = \wp' \cup \wp_c$. In the example of Fig. 4.7, the dichotomizer $h_1$ considers the sub-sets $\wp^+_1 = \{C_1, C_2\}$ and $\wp^-_1 = \{C_3\}$. Then, those positions containing class $C_1$ are replaced with $C_{11}$ and $C_{12}$. The process is repeated until the desired performance is achieved or the stopping conditions are full-filled.

The conditions that guide the learning and splitting process are defined by the set of parameters $\theta = \{\theta_{size}, \theta_{perf}, \theta_{impr}\}$, where $\theta_{size}$ corresponds to the minimum size of a sub-set to be clustered, $\theta_{perf}$ contains the minimum error desired for each binary problem, and $\theta_{impr}$ looks for the improvement of the split sub-sets regarding the previous ones. The function $TEST\_PARAMETERS$ in Algorithm 12 is responsible for testing the constraints based on the parameters $\{\theta_{size}, \theta_{perf}, \theta_{impr}\}$. If the constraints are satisfied, the new sub-sets are selected and used to recursively call the splitting function (**Step 3** of Algorithm 12). The constraints of the function $TEST\_PARAMETERS$ are fixed by default as follows:

The number of objects in $J_{\wp+}$ has to be larger than $\theta_{size}$.

The number of objects in $J_{\wp-}$ has to be larger than $\theta_{size}$.

The error $\xi(h(J_{\wp-}, J_{\wp+}))$ obtained from the dichomomizer $h$ using a particular base classifier applied on the sets $\{\wp^+, \wp^-\}$ has to be larger than $\theta_{perf}$.

The sum of the well-classified objects from the two new problems (based on the confusion matrices) divided by the total number of objects has to be greater than $1 - \theta_{impr}$.

$\theta_{size}$ avoids the learning of very unbalanced problems. $\theta_{perf}$ determines when the performance of a partition of classes is insufficient and sub-classes are required. And finally, when a partition does not obtain the desired performance $\theta_{perf}$, the splitting of the data stops, preventing overtraining.

In the example of Fig. 4.7, the three dichotomizers $h_1$, $h_2$, and $h_3$ find a solution for the problem (look the trained boundaries shown in Fig. 4.7b), obtaining a classification error under $\theta_{perf}$, so, the process stops. Now, the original tree encoding of the DECOC design shown in Fig. 4.7d can be represented by the tree structure of Fig. 4.7e, where the original class associated to each sub-class is shown in the leaves.

Summarizing, when a set of objects belonging to different classes is split, object labels are not taken into account. It can be seen as a clustering in the sense that the sub-sets are split into more simple ones while the splitting constraints are satisfied. It is important to note that when one uses different base classifiers, the sub-class splitting is probably applied to different classes or sub-classes, and therefore, the final number of sub-classes and binary problems differs.

When the final set of binary problems is obtained, its respective set of labels $\wp'$ is used to create the coding matrix $M$ (Eq. 4.10). The outputs $C'$ and $J'$ contain the final set of sub-classes and the new data for each sub-class, respectively.

Finally, to decode the new sub-class problem-dependent design of ECOC, we take advantage of the Loss-Weighted decoding design of Sect. 4.4.2.4. The decoding strategy uses a set of normalized probabilities based on the performance of the base classifier and the ternary ECOC constraints.

To show the effect of the Sub-class ECOC strategy for different base classifiers, we used the previous toy problem of the top of Fig. 4.7a. Five different base classifiers are applied: Fisher Linear Discriminant Analysis (*FLDA*), Discrete Adaboost, Nearest Mean Classifier, Linear *SVM*, and *SVM* with Radial Basis Function kernel.[4] Using these base classifiers on the toy problem, the original DECOC strategy with the Loss-Weighted algorithm obtains the decision boundaries shown on the top row of Fig. 4.8. The new learned boundaries are shown on the bottom row of Fig. 4.8 for fixed parameters $\theta$. Depending on the flexibility of the base classifier more sub-classes are required, and thus, more binary problems. Observe that all base classifiers are able to find a solution for the problem, although with different types of decision boundaries.

The selection of the set of parameters $\theta$ has a decisive influence on the final results. We can decrease the value of $\theta_{perf}$ and increase the value of $\theta_{impr}$ to obtain a better solution for a problem, but we need to optimize the parameters to avoid overtraining by stopping the procedure if no more improvement can be achieved. In the same way, sometimes to obtain the best solution for a problem implies to learn more simple problems. These points should be considered to obtain the desired trade-off between performance and computational cost. A simple example to show the evolution of learning for different parameters $\theta$ over the previous problem is shown in Fig. 4.9. The base classifier applied is *FLDA*. One can observe that when $\theta_{perf}$ decreases,

---

[4]   The parameters of the base classifiers are explained in the evaluation section.

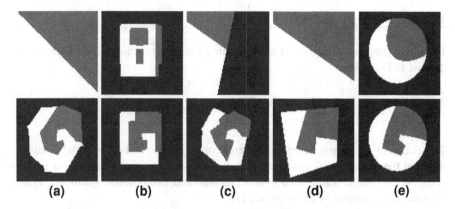

**Fig. 4.8** Sub-class ECOC without sub-classes (top) and including sub-classes (bottom): for *FLDA* **a**, Discrete Adaboost **b**, *NMC* **c**, Linear *SVM* **d**, and *RBF SVM* **e**

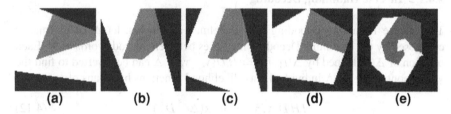

**Fig. 4.9** Learned boundaries using *FLDA* with $\theta_{size} = \frac{|J|}{50}$, $\theta_{impr} = 0.95$, and $\theta_{perf} = 0.2$ **a**, $\theta_{perf} = 0.15$ **b**, $\theta_{perf} = 0.1$ **c**, $\theta_{perf} = 0.05$ **d**, and $\theta_{perf} = 0$ **e**, respectively

more dichotomizers are required to obtain a higher performance. Thus, to achieve the desired accuracy, more sub-classes and binary problems are needed.

## 4.4 Error-Correcting Output Codes: Decoding Designs

In this section, we review the state-of-the-art on ECOC decoding designs. The decoding strategies (independently of the rules they are based on) are divided depending if they were designed to deal with the binary or the ternary ECOC frameworks.

### 4.4.1 Binary Decoding

The binary decoding designs most frequently applied are: Hamming Decoding [2], Inverse Hamming Decoding [22], and Euclidean Decoding [9].

#### 4.4.1.1 Hamming Decoding

The initial proposal to decode is the Hamming Decoding measure. This measure is defined as follows:

$$HD(x, y_i) = \sum_{j=1}^{n}(1 - sign(x^j y_i^j))/2 \tag{4.11}$$

This decoding strategy is based on the error correcting principles under the assumption that the learning task can be modeled as a communication problem, in which class information is transmitted over a channel, and two possible symbols can be found at each position of the sequence [4].

#### 4.4.1.2 Inverse Hamming Decoding

The Inverse Hamming Decoding [22] is defined as follows: let $\Delta$ be the matrix composed by the Hamming Decoding measures between the codewords of $M$. Each position of $\Delta$ is defined by $\Delta(i_1, i_2) = HD(y_{i_1}, y_{i_2})$. $\Delta$ can be inverted to find the vector containing the $N$ individual class likelihood functions by means of:

$$IHD(x, y_i) = \max(\Delta^{-1} D^T) \tag{4.12}$$

where the values of $\Delta^{-1} D^T$ can be seen as the proportionality of each class codeword in the test codeword, and $D$ is the vector of Hamming Decoding values of the test codeword $x$ for each of the base codewords $y_i$. The practical behavior of the $IHD$ showed to be very close to the behavior of the $HD$ strategy [2].

#### 4.4.1.3 Euclidean Decoding

Another well-known decoding strategy is the Euclidean Decoding. This measure is defined as follows:

$$ED(x, y_i) = \sqrt{\sum_{j=1}^{n}(x^j - y_i^j)^2} \tag{4.13}$$

### 4.4.2 Ternary Decoding

In this section we review the state-of-the-art on ternary ECOC decoding designs.

### 4.4.2.1 Loss-Based Decoding

The Loss-based decoding strategy [9] chooses the label $\ell_i$ that is most consistent with the predictions $f$ (where $f$ is a real-valued function $f : \rho \rightarrow R$), in the sense that, if the data sample $\rho$ was labeled $\ell_i$, the total loss on example $(\rho, \ell_i)$ would be minimized over choices of $\ell_i \in \ell$, where $\ell$ is the complete set of labels. Formally, given a Loss-function model, the decoding measure is the total loss on a proposed data sample $(\rho, \ell_i)$:

$$LB(\rho, y_i) = \sum_{j=1}^{n} L(y_i^j f^j(\rho)) \qquad (4.14)$$

where $y_i^j f^j(\rho)$ corresponds to the *margin* and $L$ is a Loss-function that depends on the nature of the binary classifier. The two most common Loss-functions are $L(\theta) = -\theta$ (Linear Loss-based Decoding (*LLB*)) and $L(\theta) = e^{-\theta}$ (Exponential Loss-based Decoding (*ELB*)). The final decision is achieved by assigning a label to example $\rho$ according to the class $c_i$ which obtains the minimum score.

### 4.4.2.2 Probabilistic Decoding

The authors of [23] proposed a probabilistic decoding strategy based on the continuous output of the classifier to deal with the ternary decoding. The decoding measure is given by:

$$PD(y_i, F) = -\log \left( \prod_{j\in[1,...,n]:M(i,j)\neq 0} P(x^j = M(i, j)|f^j) + K \right) \qquad (4.15)$$

where $K$ is a constant factor that collects the probability mass dispersed on the invalid codes, and the probability $P(x^j = M(i, j)|f^j)$ is estimated by means of:

$$P(x^j = y_i^j|f^j) = \frac{1}{1 + e^{y_i^j(v^j f^j + \omega^j)}} \qquad (4.16)$$

where vectors $v$ and $\omega$ are obtained by solving an optimization problem [23].

### 4.4.2.3 Attenuated Euclidean Decoding

This technique is an adaptation of the Euclidean decoding. The formulation is redefined taking into account the factors $| y_i^j || x^j |$; that makes the measure to be unaffected by the positions of the codeword $y_i$ that contain the zero symbol ($| y_i^j | = 0$). Note that in most of the cases $|x^j| = 1$. Then, the Euclidean Decoding measure is redefined as follows:

$$M = \begin{bmatrix} 1 & 1 & -1 & 0 \\ 1 & -1 & 0 & 0 \\ 1 & 1 & 1 & -1 \end{bmatrix} \quad H = \begin{bmatrix} 0.955 & 0.955 & 1.000 & 0.000 \\ 0.900 & 0.800 & 0.000 & 0.000 \\ 1.000 & 0.905 & 0.805 & 0.805 \end{bmatrix} \quad M_W = \begin{bmatrix} 0.328 & 0.328 & 0.344 & 0.000 \\ 0.529 & 0.471 & 0.000 & 0.000 \\ 0.285 & 0.257 & 0.229 & 0.229 \end{bmatrix}$$

**(a)**                                    **(b)**                                                            **(c)**

**Fig. 4.10** **a** Coding matrix $M$ of four hypotheses for a 3-class problem. **b** Performance matrix $\mathscr{H}$. **c** Weight matrix $M_W$.

$$AED(x, y_i) = \sqrt{\sum_{j=1}^{n} |y_i^j| |x^j| (x^j - y_i^j)^2} \qquad (4.17)$$

### 4.4.2.4 Loss-Weighted Decoding

The Loss-Weighted decoding is defined as a combination of normalized probabilities that weights the decoding process. We define a weight matrix $M_W$ by assigning to each position of the codeword codified by $\{-1, +1\}$ a weight of $\frac{1}{n-z}$, being $z$ the number of positions of the codeword coded by zero. Moreover, we assign a weight of zero to those positions of the weight matrix $M_W$ that contain a zero in the coding matrix $M$. In this way, $\sum_{j=1}^{n} M_W(i, j) = 1, \forall i = 1, \ldots, N$.

We assign to each position $(i, j)$ of a performance matrix $\mathscr{H}$ a continuous value that corresponds to the performance of the dichotomizer $h_j$ classifying the samples of class $c_i$ as follows:

$$\mathscr{H}(i, j) = \frac{1}{m_i} \sum_{k=1}^{m_i} \varphi(h^j(\rho_k^i), i, j), \quad \text{based on} \quad \varphi(x^j, i, j) = \begin{cases} 1, & \text{if } x^j = y_i^j, \\ 0, & \text{otherwise.} \end{cases}$$
$$(4.18)$$

Note that Eq. 4.18 makes $\mathscr{H}$ to have zero probability at those positions corresponding to unconsidered classes.

We normalize each row of the matrix $\mathscr{H}$ so that $M_W$ can be considered as a discrete probability density function:

$$M_W(i, j) = \frac{\mathscr{H}(i, j)}{\sum_{j=1}^{n} \mathscr{H}(i, j)}, \quad \forall i \in [1, \ldots, N], \quad \forall j \in [1, \ldots, n] \qquad (4.19)$$

In Fig. 4.10, a weight matrix $M_W$ for a 3-multi-class problem of four hypotheses is estimated. Figure 4.10a shows the coding matrix $M$. The matrix $\mathscr{H}$ of Fig. 4.10b represents the accuracy of the hypotheses classifying the instances of the training set. The normalization of $\mathscr{H}$ results in a weight matrix $M_W$ shown in Fig. 4.10c.

Once we compute the weight matrix $M_W$, we include this matrix in the Loss-based decoding. The decoding estimation is obtained by means of an *ELB* decoding model $L(\theta) = e^{-\theta}$, where $\theta$ corresponds to $y_i^j \cdot f(\rho, j)$ (similar to the Loss-based decoding), weighted using $M_W$[5]:

$$LW(\rho, i) = \sum_{j=1}^{n} \mathbf{M_W(i, j)} L(\mathbf{y_i^j} \cdot \mathbf{f}(\rho, \mathbf{j})) \qquad (4.20)$$

The summarized algorithm is shown in Algorithm 13.

---

**Algorithm 13** Loss-Weighted algorithm.

---

**Loss-Weighted Strategy**: Given a coding matrix $M$,

1) Calculate the performance matrix $\mathscr{H}$:

$$\mathscr{H}(i, j) = \frac{1}{m_i} \sum_{k=1}^{m_i} \varphi(h^j(\rho_k^i), \mathbf{i}, \mathbf{j}) \text{ based on } \varphi(\mathbf{x^j}, \mathbf{i}, \mathbf{j}) = \begin{cases} 1, & \text{if } x^j = y_i^j, \\ 0, & \text{otherwise.} \end{cases}$$
$$(4.21)$$

2) Normalize $\mathscr{H}$: $\sum_{j=1}^{n} M_W(i, j) = 1, \quad \forall i = 1, \ldots, N$:

$$M_W(i, j) = \frac{\mathscr{H}(i, j)}{\sum_{j=1}^{n} \mathscr{H}(i, j)}, \quad \forall i \in [1, \ldots, N], \quad \forall j \in [1, \ldots, n] \quad (4.22)$$

3) Given a test data sample $\rho$, decode based on:

$$LW(\rho, i) = \sum_{j=1}^{n} \mathbf{M_W(i, j)} L(\mathbf{y_i^j} \cdot \mathbf{f}(\rho, \mathbf{j})) \qquad (4.23)$$

---

# References

1. Jain, A., Duin, R., Mao, J.: Statistical pattern recognition: A review. IEEE Trans. Pattern Anal. Mach. Intell. 22 (2000)
2. Pelikan, M., Goldberg, D. E., Cantu-Paz, E.: Learning machines. McGraw-Hill, (1965)
3. Hastie, T., Tibshirani, R.: Classification by pairwise grouping. NIPS **26**, 451–471 (1998)
4. Dietterich, T., Bakiri, G.: Solving multiclass learning problems via error-correcting output codes. J. Artif. Intell. Res. **2**, 263–286 (1995)
5. Windeatt, T., Ardeshir, G.: Boosted ecoc ensembles for face recognition. International Conference on Visual Information Engineering 165–168 (2003)
6. Kittler, J., Ghaderi, R., Windeatt, T., Matas, T.: Face verification using error correcting output codes. CVPR **1**, 755–760 (2001)
7. Ghani, R.: Combining labeled and unlabeled data for text classification with a large number of categories. 597–598 (2001)

---

[5] Note that different Loss-functions as well as discrete and continuous outputs of the classifiers can also be applied.

8. Zhou, J., Suen, C.: Unconstrained numeral pair recognition using enhanced error correcting output coding: A holistic approach **1**, 484–488 (2005)

9. Allwein, E., Schapire, R., Singer, Y.: Reducing multiclass to binary: A unifying approach for margin classifiers. **1**, 113–141 (2002)

10. Dietterich, T., Kong, E.: Error-correcting output codes corrects bias and variance. In: Prieditis, S., Russell, S. (ed.) Proceedings of the 21th International Conference on Machine Learning, pp. 313–321, (1995)

11. Ricci, F., Aha, D.: Error-correcting output codes for local learners. European conference on machine learning **1398**, 280–291 (1998)

12. Utschick, W., Weichselberger, W.: Stochastic organization of output codes in multiclass learning problems. Neural Comput. **13**, 1065–1102 (2004)

13. Crammer, K., Singer, Y.: On the learnability and design of output codes for multi-class problems. Mach. Learn. **47**, 201–233 (2002)

14. Pujol, O., Radeva, P., Vitrià, J.: Discriminant ecoc: A heuristic method for application dependent design of error correcting output codes. Trans. PAMI **28**, 1001–1007 (2006)

15. Friedman, J., Hastie, T., Tibshirani, R.: Additive logistic regression: A statistical view of boosting. Ann. Stat. **28**(2), 337–407 (2000)

16. Torralba, A., Murphy, K., Freeman, W.: Sharing visual features for multiclass and multiview object detection. CVPR **2**, 762–769 (2004)

17. Hsu, C., Chang, C., Lin, C.: A practical guide to support vector classification. Department of CSIE. technical report (2002)

18. Zgu, Q.: Minimum cross-entropy approximation for modeling of highly intertwining data sets at subclass levels. J. Intell. Inform. Syst. **11**, 139–152 (1998)

19. Daume, H., Marcu, D.: A bayesian model for supervised clustering with the dirichlet process prior. J. Mach. Learn. Res. **6**, 1551–1577 (2005)

20. Zhu, M., Martinez, A.M.: Subclass discriminant analysis. IEEE Trans. Pattern Anal. Mach. Intell. **28**, 1274–1286 (2006)

21. Pudil, P., Ferri, F., Novovicova, J., Kittler, J.: Floating search methods for feature selection with nonmonotonic criterion functions. Proc. Int. Conf. Pattern Recognition 279–283 (1994)

22. Windeatt, T., Ghaderi, R.: Coding and decoding for multi-class learning problems. Inf. Fusion **4**, 11–21 (2003)

23. Passerini, A., Pontil, M., Frasconi, P.: New results on error correcting output codes of kernel machines. IEEE Trans. Neural Netw. **15**, 45–54 (2004)

# Chapter 5
# Traffic Sign Detection and Recognition System

**Abstract** Detection and recognition steps are the key elements of a full traffic sign system. In this chapter, a complete description of a complete traffic sign system and how the component pieces are glued together are provided. Starting with the stereo acquisition module, data are fed into an attentional cascade detection algorithm. This step is performed separately for each video source and the coherence of the detections for the stereo pair is checked. As a result the location of the traffic sign and its size if obtained. The detected signs are normalized taking into account their shape. Then, they are given to the Forest-ECOC classification stage. All stages are validated individually and as a whole providing competitive results with respect to the state-of-the-art techniques.

**Keywords** Traffic sign recognition · Mobile mapping systems · Geovan · Stereo association · Traffic sign data set · Model fitting

The methods introduced in Chaps. 3 and 4 can be used as core techniques for many general detection and recognition tasks. In this chapter, these techniques are used to define in detail a fully functional traffic sign detection and recognition system for a mobile mapping application. Starting with the system architecture, each module is described in detail, with information on the acquisition and preprocessing of data. The detection step using an attentional cascade of classifiers with dissociated dipoles is described, followed by an explanation of the classification step including details on data normalization and the classifier architecture. Finally, we report on the system validation and overall performance.

## 5.1 System Architecture

The full system architecture is shown in Fig. 5.1. It is divided into three main blocks. The first block considers data acquisition and stereo camera calibration. In the detection step, data are fed into three different attentional cascades of classifiers tuned

S. Escalera et al., *Traffic-Sign Recognition Systems*, SpringerBriefs in Computer Science, 81
DOI: 10.1007/978-1-4471-2245-6_5, © Sergio Escalera 2011

to explicitly find danger/yield, command and prohibition signs. The attentional cascade uses the concepts introduced in Chap. 3, evolutionary adaboost and dissociated dipoles. The results of these cascades are used in conjunction with the stereo calibration parameters to verify the detection in both image planes. Finally, the last block receives the regions of interest containing the detected signs. Various preprocessing pipelines are considered according to their geometry. Danger signs use a Hough transform-based preprocessing step, while the rest of the signs use a fast radial symmetry transform one. Classification is performed using the Forest-ECOC (F-ECOC) approach introduced in Chap. 4.

### 5.1.1 Acquisition Module

The mobile mapping system has a stereo pair of calibrated cameras which are synchronized with a GPS/INS system. Therefore, the result of the acquisition step is a set of stereo-pairs of images with information on their position and orientation. This information allows the use of epipolar geometry in order to change from one camera to the other and to obtain the real position in world coordinates of a point. In order to detect all signs that appear in the input image independently of their size and position, the image is scanned using windows at different scales. All these windows are used as the detector input. The detector can be defined as a classification function $h : X \mapsto \{-1, 1\}$, where $X$ is a window from the input image. The result of the detection process is a set of windows that corresponds to the valid objects, that is, all the windows $X$ where $h(X) = 1$.

### 5.1.2 Detection Module

All the data generated in the acquisition process are presented to the detector. The trained detectors are organized as an attentional cascade [1]. The *attentional cascade* is a degenerated decision tree where at each stage a detector is trained to detect almost all objects of interest while rejecting a certain fraction of the non-sign patterns. Because of the huge number of different traffic sign types, they are grouped using a similarity criterion, and a different cascade is trained for each group. Each window in the input images is analyzed by all the cascades, and the detected objects from each cascade are given as the output of the detector.

#### 5.1.2.1 Stereo Association

Since it is a stereo system, all signs appear on both cameras at each frame (except in case of occlusions or if one of the signs is out of the field of view). This redundant information is used in order to improve the detection ratio. Using the epipolar geometry, given an instance of a sign in one of the sources, the region where a sign must

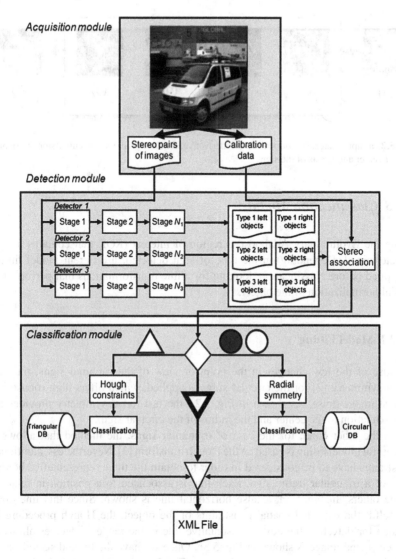

**Fig. 5.1** Scheme of the whole traffic sign recognition system

appear in the other source is estimated. Once the search window has been reduced in the other source, a similarity criterion based on normalized cross-correlation is applied. The point with the highest similarity value gives us the position of the target object. This information is used to link the object of a source with its stereo objector in order to recover it. Using this information, the only objects lost are those that have been lost in both cameras. Using the calibration data, the position and orientation information of the GPS/INS system, and the coordinates of an object in each camera, the object position in world coordinates is computed.

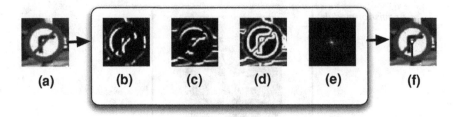

**Fig. 5.2** **a** Input image, **b** *X*-derivative, **c** *Y*-derivative, **d** image gradient, **e** accumulator of orientations, **f** center and radius of the sign

## 5.1.3  Classification Module

Using the Evolutionary Adaboost, a region of interest (ROI) that contains a sign is determined. Depending on the type of sign detected, a different model fitting is applied before classification, looking for affine transformations that perform the spatial normalization of the object.

### 5.1.3.1  Model Fitting

Because of the few changes in the point of view of the captured signs, the fast radial symmetry [2] for the circular signs is applied, which offers high robustness against image noise. As shown in Fig. 5.2 , the fast radial symmetry provides an approximation to the center and the radius of the circular sign.

On the other hand, for the case of triangular signs, the method that allows a successful model fitting is based on the Hough transform [3]. Nevertheless, additional constraints have to be considered in order to obtain the three representative border lines of a triangular traffic sign. Each line is associated to a position in relation to the others. In Fig. 5.3a, a false horizontal line is shown. Since this line does not fulfill the expected spatial constraints of the object, the Hough procedure is iterated for detecting the next representative line in the range of degrees allowed. The corrected image is shown in Fig. 5.3b. Once we have the three detected lines, their intersection is computed, as shown in Fig. 5.3c. To ensure that the lines are the expected ones, this information is complemented by looking for a corner at the circular region of each intersection surroundings (as shown in Fig. 5.3d and e) $S = \{(x_i, y_i) \mid \exists p < ((x - x_i)^2 + (y - y_i)^2 - r^2)\} \mid i \in [1, \ldots, 3]$, where $S$ is the set of valid intersection points, and $p$ corresponds to a corner point to be located in a neighborhood of the intersection point. Since at each line intersection a corner should be determined, a corner detector is applied at surroundings of the triangular vertices to increase the confidence of determining a sign.

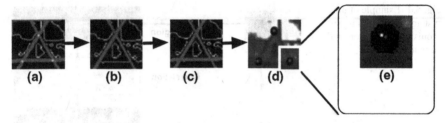

**Fig. 5.3** **a** Detected lines, **b** corrected line, **c** intersections, **d** corner region, **e** corner found

### 5.1.3.2 Spatial Normalization

Once the sign model has been fitted using the above methods, the next step is the spatial normalization of the object before classification. The steps are: a) transforming the image to make there cognition invariant to small affine deformations, b) resizing the object to the signs database size, c) filtering, using the Weickertanisotropic filter [4], and d) masking the image to exclude the background pixels at the classification step. To prevent the effects of illumination changes, the histogram equalization improves image contrast and yields a uniform histogram.

### 5.1.3.3 Classification

Once the signs are extracted, they are classified by means of the F-ECOC strategy. The optimal trees consider the best sub-partitions of classes to obtain robust classifiers based on the gray-level pixel-values of the object.

## 5.1.4 System Outputs

At the end of the system, a XML file is generated, containing the position,size, and class of each of the traffic signs detected. This information is used to obtain the real world position of each detected and recognized sign. An example of the whole process is shown in Fig. 5.4.

## 5.2 Performance Evaluation of the System

The different experiments in this section focusd on evaluating each individual part of the framework separately (detection and classification), and finally, the evaluation of the whole system.

**Fig. 5.4** Example of the system execution: image acquisition, detection, and classification

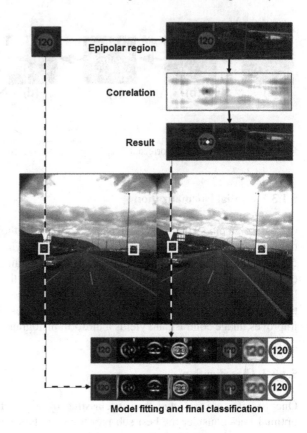

## 5.2.1 General Experimental Settings

The methodology is validated using real images from the mobile mapping system Geomobil [5]. This system captures georeferenced stereo-pairs of images, which are the input of the recognition system. For these experiments, the system was configured to acquire one frame every ten meters or when the orientation variation is greater than 60°. These parameters are thoroughly tested to ensure a correct acquisition inroad scenarios, which means that all the objects of interest appear at least in two or three stereo-pairs of images with a minimum size of 30 × 30 pixels resolution to be processed. To ensure a high diversity of road conditions, we selected three recording sessions, each one carried out on a different day in different weather conditions. It represents a total of 9.510 stereo-pairs road images. To avoid using different images containing the same traffic sign in the training and test sets, instead of using random sequences the sessions are divided in to four subsequences of similar numbers of frames, without sharing signs. The first and third parts are used to train, and the second and fourth to test. A larger test set is used because there are a great many frames that do not contain objects, and it is interesting to extract the false alarm ratio in normal conditions, testing the system under different lighting conditions, road types, and traffic intensities.

## 5.2.2 Traffic Sign Detection Results

To perform all the tests with the evolutionary Adaboost approach, we use a Genetic Algorithm with a population size of 100 individuals, Gaussian based mutation probability (the Gaussian is centered at zero with a variance of the half of the variable range, the variance decreasing over the generations), and a scattered cross-over strategy with a cross-over fraction of 0.8. When a genetic algorithm is used instead of an exhaustive search, different initializations of the algorithm with the same training data give rise to different weak classifiers. Since the dissociated dipoles cannot be learned by the classical approach, in this experiment the Haar-like features are used. A one-stage detector is learnt using fixed training and test sets, comparing the error evolution for both strategies, and the variance in the evolutionary approach over different runs. The learning process is iterated over the same training and test sets 50 times, using 50 iterations of the evolutionary Adaboost. In the case of the classic Adaboost, as the *Weak Learner* performs an exhaustive search over the features, in each round the selected features are the same. In the case of the Genetic Algorithm, the mean error value over all the rounds for each iteration is computed. In Fig. 5.5 the train and test mean error values at each iteration are shown. Note that the two methods converge with the same number of iterations. To analyze the error variability, in Fig. 5.6 the means and standard deviations for the error at each iteration are shown. The confidence interval shows that the variance is very small. Therefore, though the evolutionary Adaboost has a random component, the goodness of the given solution is similar.

### 5.2.2.1 Detector Performance

To evaluate the detector performance, a cascade of detectors is trained using the evolutionary method with ordinal dissociated dipoles. In Fig. 5.7 the most relevant features selected by the evolutionary method at the first stage of the cascade are displayed. Note that only a few of them correspond to Haar-like features. Due to the different frequency of appearance of each type of sign and the high intra-class variability, we trained a detection cascade for each group of similar signs. Table 5.1 shows the groups of signs and the number of positive samples used to train each cascade. The number of negative samples in the training process is automatically selected at each stage with a proportion of 3:1 (three negative examples for each positive example). Most of the images captured are from main roads, and consequently, some types of signs do not appear often enough to train a detector. For this reason, we only trained the four detectors shown in Table 5.1.

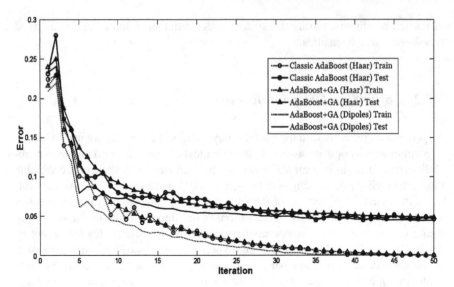

**Fig. 5.5** Error evolution using the classic Adaboost approach and the genetic Weak Learner

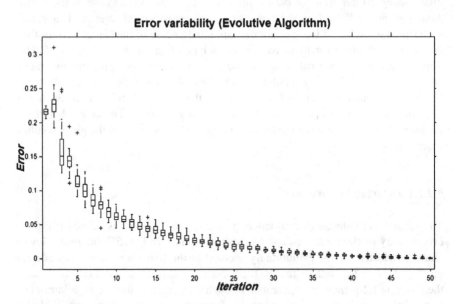

**Fig. 5.6** Genetic approach. Error variability on the training process

| **Table 5.1** Number of positive samples used to train the cascade for each considered sign | Sign | Danger | Yield | Command | Prohibition |
|---|---|---|---|---|---|
| | #Samples | 545 | 425 | 256 | 993 |

**Fig. 5.7** Some examples of the selected dipoles obtained on the danger signs

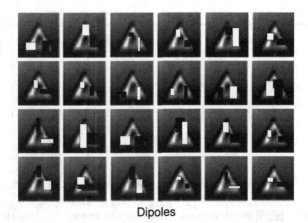

Dipoles

**Table 5.2** False alarm rates for each sign type

| Sign | Danger | Yield | Command | Prohibition |
|------|--------|-------|---------|-------------|
| FA/Sign | 2.140 | 4.549 | 8.551 | 0.696 |
| FA/Frame | 0,045 | 0,056 | 0,073 | 0,019 |

The results are analyzed using two configurations. The first uses the stereo association, to take advantage of the stereo information. The second considers each stereo-pair of images as two independent images. For each configuration, the results obtained with and without sequential information are extracted. When sequential information is used, different instances of the same real traffic sign are considered as the same object. If this information is not used, each instance is considered as an independent object. In Fig. 5.8, the hit ratio of the detector trained for each type of sign is shown. In general, observe that the accuracy of the detectors depends on the variability of sign appearance and the size of the training set. The first and the third columns correspond to the results considering each appearance of a traffic sign as a different sign. And the second and the fourth columns only take into account the real traffic signs, considering that a sign is detected if we can detect it in one or more frames where it appears. The first two columns do not account for stereo redundancy, whereas the last two columns do account for it. The other measure used for evaluating the performance of the system is the false alarm rate. In mobile mapping systems an important point is the percentage of the detected objects that effectively corresponds to traffic signs. Therefore, the false alarm value here is referred to the signs detected instead of the number of windows analyzed, which is of the order of 5,000,000 per stereo-pair. Nevertheless, the number of false positives with respect to the number of stereo-pair images has been included to simplify the analysis of the results. Both false alarm rates for each type of sign are detailed in Table 5.2. Some samples of detected objects and false alarms are shown in Fig. 5.9. One can see that the system is able to detect the signs in very extreme lighting conditions. In the false positive images, one can see that other road elements frequently look similar to traffic signs.

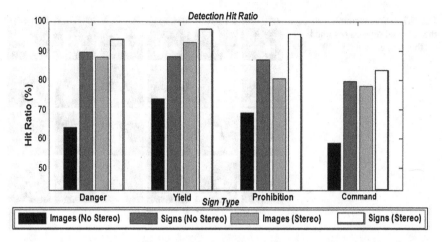

**Fig. 5.8**  Hit ratio for each sign type, using dissociated dipoles

**Fig. 5.9**  Some samples
of detected objects (true
positives) and false positives

## 5.2.3  Traffic Sign Recognition Results

This section shows the performance of the traffic sign classification using different
state-of-the-art classifiers. First of all, we discuss the generation of the database to
train the classifiers and to perform the experiments. We then report the classification
results considering three groups of traffic signs. Finally, we give the results of the
full classification framework including model fitting and classification.

### 5.2.3.1  Classification Database

The database used to train the classifiers was designed using the regions of interest
obtained from the detection step and the model fitting methods presented in the
previous sections. Three groups of classes are defined using the most common types
of signs. The classes considered are shown in Fig. 5.10. Speed signs need special

**Fig. 5.10** Set of classes considered in the classification module, i.e. speed classes, circular classes, and triangular classes

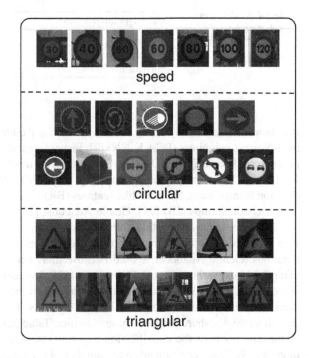

**Table 5.3** Characteristics of the databases usedfor classification. The training and test examples are equally distributed among the group classes

| Dataset | #Training examples | #Test examples | #Features | #Classes |
|---------|---------|---------|---------|---------|
| Circular | 750 | 200 | 1225 | 12 |
| Speed | 500 | 200 | 1681 | 7 |
| Triangular | 750 | 200 | 1716 | 12 |

attention. These types of signs are less discriminatory as some of them are only differentiable by a few pixels. With this type of sign it is better to work on binary images to avoid the errors that may accumulate because of the gray levels of the signs. For the 12 classes of circular signs and 12 classes of triangular signs, a set of 750 training images is considered in both cases. For the seven speed classes a set of 500 training samples is used. Finally, the resolution of each database is: $35 \times 35$ pixels for the circular group, $44 \times 39$ pixels for the triangular group, and $41 \times 41$ pixels for the speed group respectively.

### 5.2.3.2 Traffic Sign Classification

To evaluate the F-ECOC performance, we compare it with the state-of-the-art classifiers. The details for each strategy are: 3-Euclidean distance nearest neighbors (K-NN), Tangent distance(TD) [6] with invariant tangent vector with respect to

**Table 5.4** Model fitting and
classification results

| Recognition problem | Accuracy |
|---|---|
| Circular | 98.00 |
| Speed | 91.50 |
| Triangular | 92.50 |

translation, rotation, and scaling, 99.98% of Principal components analysis followed by 3-Nearest neighbors (PCA K-NN) [7], Fisher linear discriminant analysis with a previous 99.98% PCA (FLDA) [7], Support vector machine with projection kernel Radial basis function and the parameter $\gamma = 1$ (SVM) [8], Gentle Adaboost with decision stumps using the Haar-like features (BR) [9, 10], multi class joint boosting with decision stumps (JB) [11], Gentle Adaboost [12] sampling with FLDA (BS), statistical gentle naive boosting with decision stumps (NB) [10], and our F-ECOC with 3-embedded optimal trees. In the different variants of boosting we apply 50 iterations. Gentle Adaboost is used because ithas been shown to outperform the other Adaboost variants in real applications [12]. As regards the F-ECOC base classifier, FLDA is used in the experiments classifying traffic signs and 50 runs of gentle Adaboost with decision stumps on the UCI data sets. This last choice was made so that all strategies share the same base classifier. Table 5.3 shows the characteristics of the data used for the classification experiments, where #Training, #Test, #Features, and #Classes correspond to the number of training and test samples, number of features, and number of classes respectively.

The classification results and confidence intervals are shown graphically in Fig. 5.11 for the different groups. One can see that the F-ECOC using FLDA as a base classifier attains the highest accuracy in all cases. Nevertheless, for the circular and triangular signs the differences among classifiers are significant because of the high discriminability of these two groups. The speed group is a more difficult classification problem. In this case, the F-ECOC strategy obtains an accuracy of above 90%, outperforming the rest of classifiers.

### 5.2.3.3  Model Fitting Classification

Finally, to test the performance of the classification step of the system, the model fitting and F-ECOC classification are applied in a set of 200 regions of interests for each group. The regions of interest are obtained from the detection step. The results are shown in Table 5.4. One can see that for circular and speed signs the results are practically from the same as in the previous experiments. For triangular signs, the accuracy is slightly decreased because of the effect of noise, the variability of the sign appearance, and resolution, which makes the Hough transform lose some sides of the triangular signs. Nevertheless, the final results are above 90% in all cases.

**Fig. 5.11** Classification
results for the speed, circular,
and triangular problems

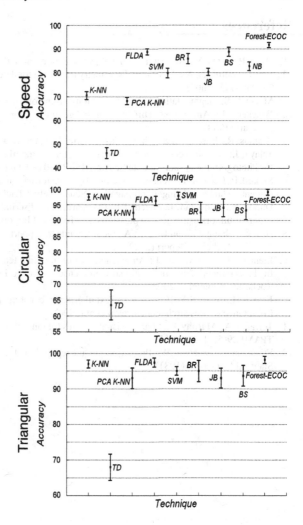

### 5.2.3.4 System Results

Performance of the whole system is computed over a test set of 10.000 stereo-pairs of images, which correspond to100 km of road. The accuracy of the real traffic sign recognition system applying the detection and classification approaches jointly obtains a mean triangular sign reliability of 90.87 ± 0.87%, and a circular sign reliability of 90.16 ± 1.01%. In the detection stage, recognition failures are due to the background confusion (see Fig. 5.9) and the high inter-class variability, whereas in the classification stage the errors are due to the poor resolution of the images.

# References

1. Viola, P., Jones, M.: Robust real-time object detection. Int. J. Comput. Vis. **57**, 137–154 (2002)
2. Loy, G., Zelinsky, A.: A fast radial symmetry transform for detecting points of interest. TPAMI **25**, 959–973 (2003)
3. Morse, B.S.: Segmentation (edge based, Hough transform). Technical Report (2000)
4. Weickert, J.: Anisotropic Diffusion in Image processing. ECMI Series, Teubner-Verlag, Stuttgart (1998)
5. Alamús, R., Baron, A., Bosch, E., Casacuberta, J., Miranda, J., Pla, M., Snchez, S., Serra, A., Talaya, J.: On the accuray and performance of the geomobil system. In: International Society for Photogrammetry and Remote Sensing (ISPRS '04), Istanbul, July 2004
6. Simard, P., LeCum, Y., Denker, J., Victorri, B.: Transformation invariance in pattern recognition, tangent distance and tangent propagation. Neural Netw.: Tricks Trade **1524**, 239–274 (1998)
7. Dudoit, S., Fridlyand, J., Speed, T.P.: Comparition of discrimination methods for the classification of tumors using gene expression data. Technical Report, June 2000
8. Hsu, C., Chang, C., and Lin, C.: A practical guide to support vector classification. Department of CSIE, Technical Report (2002)
9. Lienhart, R., and Maydt, J.: An extended set of haar-like features for rapid object detection. In: Proceedings of the International Conference on Image Processing, pp. 900–903. IEEE, Rochester, September 2002
10. Kim, Y.H., Hahn, S.Y., Zhang, B.T.: Text filtering by boosting nave bayes classifiers. In: SIGIR Conference on Research and Development (2000)
11. Torralba, A., Murphy, K.: Sharing visual features for multiclass and multiview object detection. TPAMI **29**(5), 1–16 (2007)
12. Friedman, J., Stuetzle, W.: Projection pursuit regression. J. Amer. Statist. Assoc. 76 Report, Stanford University (1981)

# Chapter 6
# Conclusion

**Abstract** Traffic sign recognition is a first step on the way to developing context-aware cars. But this context cannot be reduced to traffic signs, even if we are talking about visual information. Cars should be able to understand current conditions and to interpret visual information in a context-situated way. In this scenario, traffic signs are just another source of information and the presence of pedestrians or the evaluation of road condition are essential cues for taking the most appropriate decisions. The context-based approach to traffic sign perception stands as valuable application of advanced computer vision and for this reason in the coming years we are likely to see a great many interesting scientific results in this area.

Road sign detection is currently a robust technology for the most common signs. In the future, it will also be possible to detect more complex road signs, such as warning panels, and many others, by reading and understanding written text. One day it will also be possible to interpret special scenarios via a combination with digital maps and online traffic data, and these networked systems will be critical in improving traffic flow and decreasing congestion. For all these reasons, computer vision research will continue to have a large impact in car development and traffic management.

Traffic sign recognition is a first step on the way to developing context-aware cars. But this context cannot be reduced to traffic signs, even if we are talking about visual information. Cars should be able to understand current conditions and to interpret visual information in a context-situated way. In this scenario, traffic signs are just another source of information, and the presence of pedestrians or the evaluation of road condition are essential cues for taking the most appropriate decisions. This valuable information is only available via the use of advanced computer vision techniques which are still limited to the research laboratories.

For all these reasons, computer vision research will continue to have a large impact on car development and traffic management. Cars will be fitted with multiple cameras for evaluating their external and internal contexts. This objective needs coordinated

S. Escalera et al., *Traffic-Sign Recognition Systems*, SpringerBriefs in Computer Science, 95
DOI: 10.1007/978-1-4471-2245-6_6, © Sergio Escalera 2011

research on a range of problems; person detection and pose classification, facial expression analysis, pedestrian detection, car/bicycle detection and tracking, real-time 3D reconstruction, etc. Most of these technologies are not mature enough for technological transfer and in the coming years we are likely to see a great many interesting scientific results in these areas.